Pocket Pantheon

ALAIN BADIOU

Pocket Pantheon

Figures of Postwar Philosophy

Translated by David Macey

VERSO

London • New York

This edition first published by Verso 2009
© Verso 2009
Translation David Macey © 2009
First published as *Petit panthéon portatif*
© Editions La Fabrique 2008
All rights reserved

The moral rights of the author and translator have been asserted

1 3 5 7 9 10 8 6 4 2

Verso
UK: 6 Meard Street, London W1F 0EG
USA: 20 Jay Street, Suite 1010, Brooklyn, NY 11201
www.versobooks.com

Verso is the imprint of New Left Books

ISBN-13: 978-1-84467-357-5

British Library Cataloguing in Publication Data
A catalogue record for this book is available from the British Library

Library of Congress Cataloging-in-Publication Data
A catalog record for this book is available
from the Library of Congress

Typeset by Hewer Text UK Ltd, Edinburgh
Printed in the USA by Maple Vail

Contents

Overture

I at first thought of calling this set of tributes to philosophers who are no longer with us 'Funeral Orations'. Whilst that title is not cheerful, it does cover a famous literary history. It is, however, inaccurate. Whenever I speak of these friends, enemies and partners in a complicated game, my reading, my battles and my enthusiasms, my feelings are not those of Bossuet – a writer of immense importance but one who wrote in the service of Power. I cannot obey his injunction to pray, exemplify or even pass judgement. And so when Eric Hazan suggested the present title, I agreed almost without thinking about it, mainly because it seemed to me to be a tonic and far removed from death.[1] Now, I hold the view that neither death nor depression should be of interest to us.

1 Editorial note: Jacques-Bénigne Bossuet (1627–1704) was a French bishop and theologian, renowned for his funeral orations and sermons. Eric Hazan, founder-director of Editions La Fabrique, published this book as *Petit panthéon portatif*.

If philosophy serves any purpose, it is to take away the chalice of sad passions and to teach us that pity is not a loyal affect, that our plaints do not mean that we are right, and that victimhood is not the starting point for thought. On the one hand, and as Plato teaches us once and for all, licit passions and all creations with a universal intent originate in Truth, which, if need be, can go by the name of Beauty or the Good. On the other hand, as Rousseau knew, the human animal is essentially good, and when it is not, that is because some external cause forces it to be evil, and that cause must be detected, rooted out and destroyed as quickly as possible and without the least hesitation.

Those who claim that the human animal is wicked simply want to tame it and turn it into a morose wage-earner or depressed consumer who helps capital to circulate. Given their ability to create eternal truths in various worlds, men have within them the angel that religions saw as their double. That is what philosophy, in the true sense of the word, has always taught us. Before that inner angel can manifest its presence, it must have a principle or maxim, and ultimately it is always the same, even though it can take a wide variety of forms. Let us choose Mao's: 'Cast away illusions, prepare for struggle.'[2] Hold to the truth, cast away illusions, and fight rather than surrender, whatever the circumstances. In my view, there is only one true philosophy, and the philosophies of the fourteen whose names find shelter in my little pantheon would not want anything more.

The trouble is that, nowadays, the word 'philosophy' is used in an attempt to force upon us quite the opposite maxim, which might read: 'Cling to your illusions, prepare to surrender.' We have seen a 'philosophy' appearing in magazines that looks like a vegetable-based natural medicine, or euthanasia for enthusiasts. Philosophizing would appear to be a small part of a vast programme: keep fit and be efficient, but stay cool. We have seen 'philosophers' declaring that, as the Good is inaccessible if not criminal, we should be content to fight every inch of the way against various forms of Evil, whose common name proves, on closer inspection, to be 'communism', when it is not 'Arab' or 'Islam'. And so we revive 'values' that philosophy has always helped us to get rid of: obedience (to commercial contracts), modesty (in the face of the arrogance of the ham actor

2 'Cast Away Illusions, Prepare for Struggle', in *Selected Works of Mao Tse-Tung*, Vol. IV, Peking: Foreign Languages Press, 1969.

on TV), realism (we must have profits and inequalities), utter selfishness (now known as 'modern individualism'), colonial superiority (the democratic goodies of the West versus the despotic baddies of the South), hostility to living thought (all opinions have to be taken into account), the cult of numbers (the majority are always right), obtuse millenarianism (the planet is getting hotter under my very feet), empty religion (there must be Something), and I could go on. So many 'philosophers' and 'philosophies' do nothing to stop this, and instead wear themselves out trying to infect us with little articles, debates, blazing headlines ('The Ethics of Stock Options: Philosophers Speak Out At Last') and boisterous roundtable discussions ('Philosophers: the G-string or the Veil?'). This permanent prostitution of the words 'philosopher' and 'philosophy' (and it should be recalled that Deleuze denounced it from the very beginning), and the media operation that gave birth to the trademark 'new philosophies', will get you down in the long run. At the rate things are going, it is not just cafés that will be described as 'philosophical' (these *cafés philosophiques* really are a wretched invention, and the natural heirs to the *cafés du commerce* where all that bar room philosophizing used to go on). We will end up going, in all our pomp, to the philosophical outhouse.

So, yes, it would be right and proper to recall what a philosopher is. And to remind ourselves by looking at the examples of those who adopted that title in recent decades. We have to call them to our rescue to clean up and give a new lustre to the words in whose name they propose, with great difficulty and under great intellectual tension, to accept unconditionally the need to find at least one true Idea and never to give in, whatever the consequences, and even though, as Mallarmé said of *Igitur*, the act for which no one claims responsibility 'is perfectly absurd [except that] the infinite has at last been fixed [*fixé*]'.

Basically, I am calling my philosophical friends who are no longer with us as witnesses for the prosecution in the case the infinite is bringing against the falsifiers. They have come to say, through the voice that eulogizes them, that the imperative of contemporary democratic materialism – 'Live without Ideas' – is both cheap and inconsistent.

These texts are very different in form and intent. They are all tributes to great minds, often paid to mark their passing, the anniversary of their passing or a colloquium devoted to their memory. The texts are collected here in the order of the philosophers' date of birth. Whilst these tributes range from short essays to lengthy meditations, the differences between them have no hierarchical meaning whatsoever in this context. And besides, the final pages give not only the date and provenance of these short texts but also a little supplementary information about my intellectual relationship with the philosophers I talk about.

Whilst some of them were the masters of my youth, I would not say today that I unreservedly agree with them as to how it was constructed. I had ties of friendship with some, and a few quarrels with others. But I am glad to say here that, given the potions they are trying to make us swallow today . . . well, I love all these fourteen dead philosophers. Yes, I love them.

Jacques Lacan (1901–1981)

The man who has just died was all the greater in that greatness is becoming rare – very rare – in our uncertain lands. The media let him see that very clearly, as their goal is always to align that which exists with the transient and limited prose of journalism. They all asked his sworn enemies and those who go through the dustbins to say something about him.

When not even death can silence envy, it really is a sign of just how barbaric our societies are. All those psychoanalytic dwarves, all those gossip columnists amplifying the mean cry of 'He was standing in my way, and now he's dead at last. Now pay some attention to ME!'

It is a fact that Lacan was on the warpath right from the start, denouncing the illusory consistency of the 'Ego', rejecting the American psychoanalysis of the 1950s which proposed to 'reinforce the ego' and thereby adapt people to the social consensus and arguing that, because it is symbolically determined by language, the subject is irreducibly the subject of desire, and as such cannot be adapted to reality, except perhaps in the imaginary.

Lacan in effect established that the cause of desire is an object that has been lost, that is lacking, and that, being articulated under the symbolic law, desire has no substance and no nature. It has only a truth.

He made money out of this particularly bleak vision of psychoanalysis, in which it is the truth and not happiness that is in play, thanks to the practice of what were sometimes very short sessions. The crucial and non-existent role of psychoanalysts in the plural is to let shine – with a searingly subjective brightness – the signifier of a break that lets slip the truth of desire, whilst the individual psychoanalyst must, ultimately, reconcile himself to be nothing more than what is left at the end of the analysis and when that work is done.

The practice of short sessions polarized a real hatred of the truth against Lacan. As a result, he was literally excommunicated by the psychoanalytic International. The need to organize the transmission of his thought, and to train analysts who would act in accordance with what he believed to be the ethics of psychoanalytic practice, led him to found his own school. But even

there, the splits and dissolutions were testimony to
a stubborn reluctance to hold the severe position he
promoted to the end.

It had become good form to state that the ageing
Lacan was no longer transmitting anything worthwhile
from the 1970s onwards. In my view, it is quite the
opposite. Having lamented the theory of the subject's
subservience to the signifying rule, Lacan made one final
effort to pursue his investigation into its relationship
with the real as far as he could. The rules of the signifier
were no longer enough. What was needed was some
kind of geometry of the unconscious, a new way of
representing the three agencies (symbolic, imaginary,
real) in which the subject-effect is deployed. Lacan's
recourse to topology was an internal requirement born
of this new stage in his thinking, and it brought out his
underlying materialism.

Lacan held that politics has no effect on the real. He
used to say that 'the social is always a wound'. And yet
it so happens that even a Marxism in crisis cannot avoid
making reference to the dialectic of the subject that he
outlines. It is in effect clear that the fiasco of the Party-
States that emerged from the Third International opens
up radical questions about the essence of the political

subject. Now, neither the subject-as-consciousness (Sartre's thesis) nor the subject-as-natural substance will do. The at once divided and errant subject theorized by Lacan in his own realm does offer us a way out of that impasse. For such a subject is a product of a break, and not of the idea that it represents a reality, not even that of the working class. For today's French Marxists, the function of Lacan is the function that Hegel served for the German revolutionaries of the 1840s.

Given the trite situation in which we find ourselves, marked by the platitudes and relative self-abasement of our intellectuals, the death of Lacan, coming so soon after that of Sartre, does nothing to improve matters. We were anxious to hear what he might still have to say. Quite aside from the content of his teaching, he developed an ethics of thought that is now highly unusual.

Le Perroquet[1] will of course come back to the almost incalculable import of that ethics. For the moment, the important thing is, without any restrictions or any presumption, to pay tribute to one who is no longer with us.

1   See 'A Note on the Texts', below.

Georges Canguilhem (1904–1995)
Jean Cavaillès (1903–1944)

We will celebrate here, in the ancient manner, the celebration of dead masters by living masters. In doing so, we twice break the rule of our rapid societies, which worship what is supposedly a studied casualness. We forget our dead as quickly as we can because we are in a hurry to outlive them in our flabbiness, and we mock the masters who rejected journalism and sloganizing – 'anti-elitist' – representations of intellectual democracy.

Georges Canguilhem was – and therefore still is, for there can be no appeal against such an inscription – the strong and discreet master of my philosophical generation. Why did this specialist in the history of the life sciences exert an academic authority that could not have been further removed from his infinitely precise thought? Probably because his conception of intellectual rigour extended, on the one hand, to a minutely detailed account of the history of concepts and, on the other, to the pure logic of commitment. As a result, Canguilhem, a believer in the conception of a perennial liberal university, who was more inclined than anyone else to tell the difference between what is valid and mere semblance, extended his attention far beyond the specialist areas of knowledge in which he excelled, with an almost forgotten excellence, to everything that combines the articulated meaning of history with the ethics of action.

The sort of elective hold he had therefore made Georges Canguilhem the master of a host of disparate young philosophers whose destiny took them far away both from themselves and from him, especially when May '68 destroyed for ever the university edifice that communicated the kind of authority to which, as was only right, he insisted on remaining loyal.

We can assume two things:

First, that Canguilhem is already a great classic, and is designated as such in his works,[1] all of which

1   Some of the works of Georges Canguilhem (all published by Vrin): *Knowledge of Life* [*La Connaissance de la vie*, 1965] trans. Stefanos Geroulanos and Daniela Ginsburg, New York: Fordham University Press, 2008; *Etudes d'histoire et de philosophie des sciences* (1969); *Ideology and Rationality in*

are constructed around sequences of crucial articles that extend – or complete – the great national tradition of an epistemology supported by the historical examination of the genealogy of concepts, of breaks between the fields in which they operate, of conflicts of interpretations and of the reshaping of domains. Canguilhem is therefore to the life sciences what Koyré and Bachelard are to physics. And what Jean Cavaillès and Albert Lautman, Resistance fighters killed by the Nazis, were beginning to be for mathematics.

But there is also something that cannot be transmitted, except in the particularity of its objects, namely the subjective function of authority that Canguilhem represented. As a result, the life and work of the master went on, thank God, and the conditions, both institutional and intellectual, that related that function

---

the History of the Life Sciences, trans. Arthur Goldhammer, Cambridge, MA: MIT Press, 1988 [*Idéologie et rationalité dans l'histoire des sciences de la vie*, 1981]. Editorial note: see also, *The Normal and the Pathological*, trans. Carolyn R. Fawcett, New York: Zone Books, 1991, and *A Vital Rationalist: Selected Writings of Georges Canguilhem*, edited by François Delaporte, trans. Arthur Goldhammer, New York: Zone Books, 1994.

to our multiple eagerness for knowledge between 1950 and 1967 remained intact.

Or, I am thinking of the little book entitled *Vie et mort de Jean Cavaillès*,[2] precisely because it was not written in a scholarly register and attempts, but with a harsh simplicity, to pay homage to a murdered philosopher–resistance fighter, and because it can communicate to those of a different age something of the lost secret of the masters.

This little book brings together three texts that belong to a genre whose obsolescence will lead astray only those who consent in advance to being destroyed by the barbarism of our times: the official ceremony in honour of a great man who has died.

Mao Zedong did not go in for modern ironies and held that 'When anyone in our ranks who has done some useful work dies, be he soldier or cook, we should have a funeral ceremony and a memorial meeting in his honour.'[3]

---

2 Georges Canguilhem, *Vie et mort de Jean Cavaillès*, Paris: Editions Allia. First published in 1976 in a limited and numbered edition of 464 copies.
3 'Serve the People', in *Selected Works of Mao Tse-Tung*, Vol. III, Peking: Foreign Languages Press, 1967.

We have here the inauguration of the Amphithéâtre Jean-Cavaillès in Strasbourg (1967), a commemoration on Radiodiffusion-télévision française (1969) and a commemoration at the Sorbonne (1974). In them, Canguilhem sums up the life of Jean Cavaillès: philosopher and mathematician, teacher of logic, cofounder of the 'Libération-Sud' liberation movement, founder of the 'Cohors' military action network, arrested in 1942, escaped, arrested again in 1943, tortured and shot. Found in a common grave in a corner of the citadel in Arras, and immediately baptized 'Unknown Man 5'.[4]

But what Canguilhem is trying to reconstruct goes beyond the obvious naming of a hero ('A philosopher-mathematician carrying explosives, lucid and rash, resolute but without any optimism. If that is not a hero, what is a hero?'). Faithful, basically, to his

4   Works by Jean Cavaillès: 'Remarques sur la formation de la théorie abstraite des ensembles' (1938), 'Transfini et continue' (1943) and 'La Correspondance Cantor–Dedekind' are collected in *Philosophie mathématique*, Paris: Hermann, 1962; *Sur la logique et la théorie de la science*, Paris: Vrin, 1976 (3rd edn); *Méthode axiomatique et formalisme*, Paris: Hermann, 1938.

methodology of seeking coherence, Canguilhem is trying to decipher the link between the philosophy of Cavaillès, his commitment, and his death.

It is true that it appears to be an enigma, as Cavaillès had nothing to do with the political theory of committed existentialism; Cavaillès worked on pure mathematics. What is more, he thought that the philosophy of mathematics must rid itself of all reference to a constituent mathematical subject, and should examine the internal necessity of mathematical notions. The final sentence in his essay 'Sur la logique et la théorie de la science' (written when he was first imprisoned in the camp at St-Paul d'Eygaux on the orders of the Pétainist State), which has become famous, argues that the philosophy of consciousness must be replaced by the dialectic of concepts. To that extent, Cavaillès anticipated by twenty years what the philosophers of the 1960s were trying to do.

And it is precisely in that demand for rigour, in this educated cult of necessity, that Canguilhem sees the unity between Cavaillès's commitment and his practice as a logician. Because, having learned from Spinoza, Cavaillès wanted to de-subjectify knowledge and because he also regarded resistance as an unavoidable necessity that no reference to the Ego could circumvent. In 1943, he therefore declared: 'I am a follower of Spinoza, and I think that we can see necessity everywhere. The logical deductions of mathematicians are necessary. The stages of mathematical science are necessary. And the struggle we are waging is necessary'.

Unburdened of any reference to himself, Cavaillès therefore practised extreme forms of resistance, going so far as to enter the Kriegsmarine's submarine base in Lorient dressed in a workman's overalls, in the same way that one does science with an understated tenacity. Death is no more than one possible and neutral conclusion because, as Spinoza states, 'A free man thinks of nothing less than death, and his wisdom is a meditation on life, not on death.'[5]

As Canguilhem says: 'Cavaillès was a resistance fighter for reasons of logic.' And that assertion is all the stronger in that we can assume that Canguilhem, who remains silent about this point, was, despite

5   Benedict de Spinoza, *Ethics*, trans. Edwin Curley, London: Penguin, 1996, p. 151.

himself, as we know, also active in the Resistance for more or less the same reasons. As a result, he can legitimately mock those who, although they philosophize about the personality, ethics or consciousness, 'talk so much about themselves only because only they can talk about their resistance, given that it was so discreet'.

We probably have a clear enough idea of why Georges Canguilhem is in a position to point out to us what philosophical authenticity is. It is not about politics, and our differences would probably have become obvious, but about what makes politics a universal possibility: being able to attach so little importance to oneself even though an undeniable historic cause demands our devotion. If we do not meet that demand, we sacrifice not only our dignity, but all ethics and, ultimately, all logic and therefore all thought.

The order of thought means nothing without the irrepressible demand that founds its subjective consistency. The lesson is not pointless at a time when Polish workers are themselves giving a name to their resistance and when war is once more stalking the world.

It is therefore right, and opportune, to pay tribute to Canguilhem as he pays tribute to Cavaillès, and, of course, to be thankful to both of them, given that, to cite Spinoza once more, 'Only free men are very thankful to one another.'[6]

6   Ibid., p. 153.

Jean-Paul Sartre (1905–1980)

Sartre was involved in three great political struggles. It was thanks to them that he became the emblematic figure of the progressive intellectual everyone in the movement mourns today, whilst everyone on the side of reaction denounces him for what they call his mistakes, perversions or crimes. In the 1950s, and in the face of hysterical anti-communism and pro-Americanism, Sartre took the side of the Parti Communiste Français on the grounds that it was the sole expression of the working class. In the 1960s, Sartre supported the anti-imperialist struggle. He opposed the colonial war in Algeria. He discovered the popular power of the peoples of the Third World. In the early 1970s, or after May '68, Sartre came to understand the reactionary character of the PCF. Together with the Maoists of the day, he took the side of the immigrants, the unskilled factory workers, the miners of the Nord *département*, and of anti-capitalist and anti-union struggles.

Thirty years of correctness in revolt, well-judged changes of position, and the anger appropriate to them. And all bathed in unchallenged international glory. In terms of our literary history, the only comparison is with Voltaire, the literary prince of the eighteenth century who defended Calas, Sirven and the chevalier de la Barre; Rousseau, the best-selling novelist whose *Social Contract* was burned; and Victor Hugo, a living historical monument who was almost the only artist and intellectual to protest against the coup d'état of 2 December, and then the repression of the Commune. They are our great national writers. They combine a vast readership, a glorious status, a refusal to bow before anyone, and a freedom of movement in revolt that has never been crushed. They are writers who never surrender.

If there is something enigmatic about Sartre, it is not, as they say today, the fact that he marched side by side with the Stalinists in the 1950s. Quite the contrary: for him, that was the moment of a real conversion. Whilst he did not really have any illusions about the PCF, Sartre realized at that time that the choices facing intellectuals were historically situated. Anyone who claimed to be able to remain neutral had simply chosen to side with the forces of social conservatism. When he said that 'an anti-communist is a dog', he was simply recognizing the necessity of political reality. In 1950, it was quite true that an anti-communist had simply abdicated his responsibility and chosen servitude and oppression, both for himself and for others. It was that historical, limited nature of choice that wrested Sartre away from the metaphysics of individual salvation.

We can pinpoint the moment of that conversion – and it was both pure and confused – in his play *Lucifer and the Lord.* Goetz wanted to be the hero of Good, and then he wanted to be the hero of Evil. But that formal ethics led to disaster in the Germany of the Peasants' Revolt. Goetz therefore rejoined the peasant army, with one specific task in mind: winning the war. Like Stalin, he ruled that army, which was threatened by divisions amongst the peasants, through terror. These are Goetz's final words:

> I shall make them hate me, because I know no other way of loving them. I shall give them their orders, since I have no other way of being obeyed. I shall remain alone with this empty sky above me, since

I have no other way of being among men. There is this war to fight, and I will fight it.[1]

From that point onwards, Sartre remained convinced that there was always *some* war to fight. In 1950, he still thought that being alone was the only way of being among men, and that was a trace of his past. But he was about to change. The important thing is that, in 1950, Sartre became the man of specific commitments, the man of concrete historical conflicts. They were the three great struggles of which I spoke. That is the logic – the profound logic – of Sartre.

The enigmatic thing about Sartre came before that. There was one struggle he missed, and which did not really revolutionize either his practical attitude or his philosophy: the struggle waged by the anti-Nazi Resistance. Sartre came to politics between 1945 and 1950. It was metaphysics and art that initially made him famous. That is because Sartre elaborated his first philosophy in wartime. *Being and Nothingness* was published in 1943. There is a huge gulf between that philosophy and political commitment. Sartre made the

1 Jean-Paul Sartre, *Lucifer and the Lord*, in *Two Plays*, trans. Kitty Black, Harmondsworth: Penguin, 1965, p. 190.

absolute freedom of the Subject central to experience, and that freedom is still strictly a matter of individual consciousness. The relationship with the Other is certainly a given which constitutes that consciousness. But my relationship with the Other is what makes me see myself, through the gaze of the Other, as a shameful thing, as reduced to the being that, because I am free, I am not. The immediate relationship with the Other therefore oscillates between masochism, which allows me to make myself be for the other, and sadism, in which I make the other in order to be me. In both cases, freedom makes a point of becoming limed in being, either because I deny it in myself, or because I deny it in the other. The reversibility that allows freedoms to flee one another means that there is no room for any reciprocity or combative solidarity. The Subject is freedom's never-ending flight from being, and man is hell for man. From that perspective, no political cause can unite consciousnesses in any collective project. All unification is external: it is a form of being that itself refers to a great Other, to an invisible gaze for which we are things, and we freely accept that we are things. Any collective project can therefore only be passive. Only the individual is an active centre. Even in 1960,

Sartre would describe as 'collective' a multiplicity of individuals whose unity is a passive synthesis.

And yet from the end of the 1940s onwards, Sartre's immense effort revolved around just one question: how can activity, the only model for which is the free individual consciousness, be a collective given? How can we escape the idea that any historical and social reality is inevitably passive? The outcome of this effort was the appearance, in 1960, of the *Critique of Dialectical Reason*.

The paradox is that, in the meantime, things had taken a very different turn. Althusser wanted to restore Marxism's cutting edge by rejecting Sartre's entire frame of reference and eliminating all reference to a historical subject. By insisting on the structural character of Marxist analyses. By emphasizing scientificity, which Sartre approached only with circumspection? That was the path that was initially taken by living Marxism, but it was not Sartre's path. The Maoists of the late 1960s were to combine Marxist rigour with the historical experience of the Cultural Revolution in China. They laid claim to the cutting edge of science as a theoretical equivalent to the cutting edge of rebellion.

But with hindsight, it might also be said that, after May '68 and perhaps even more so today, political

subjectivation appears to be the central item on
Marxism's balance sheet. It takes the form of a twofold
question:

What independent revolutionary activity are the
masses capable of? Can they, as Maoism puts it, be
'self-reliant'? What is the relationship between the
mass movement and the great inert political institutions
of imperialism: parliament and the trade unions?

What political party does the working class need
today? What is the essence of the constituted political
subject?

Hence the return, if you like to put it that way, to
Sartre's basic concern. Although, to go one step further,
we could also say: the Subject that we inevitably talk
about today is not the subject of History. The idea of a
historical totalization is no longer of any use to us. We
are talking about a very specific subject: the political
subject. So Sartre's question is not exactly the right
question. All this means that summing up what he was
attempting to do is very complex.

First of all, we find in Sartre some astonishing
historical and concrete descriptions of social ensembles.
He identifies three main types: the series, which is an
inert gathering; the group, which is collective freedom

and reciprocity; and the organization, which is a serial form that has been internalized by the group.

The series is the collective form of social inertia. What Sartre calls 'inorganic social beings'. The series is a gathering of men in which every man is alone because he is interchangeable with every other man. Sartre's initial example is that of a queue at a bus stop: everyone is there for the same reason, but that common interest brings people together externally. That externality is internalized in the form of everyone's indifference to everyone else: I do not speak to the others, and simply wait in the same way that they wait. In a series men are, if you like, brought together by the object. The unity of the gatherings exists because everyone's relationship with the object is the same. But that external identity becomes an internal alterity: if the object makes me the same as everyone else, then I am other than myself. As Sartre puts it: 'Everyone is the same as the Others to the extent that he is Other than himself.' Ultimately, the law of the series is unity through separation. Sartre extends this formula to all collective activities: working on an assembly line or in local government, listening to the radio – in all these cases, the object produces an undifferentiated unity or a unity based upon separation. Typically, this is a passive synthesis. It is the moment when material production has a retroactive impact upon individual praxes and totalizes them into inertia. The human unity of the series is a unity that is grounded in impotence: being identical with the Other, everyone is external to himself and therefore cut off from free practice. The series is the rule of the Other. At which point, Sartre rediscovers one of Marxism's great ideas: the impotence of the people is always its internal division, its separation from itself. And it is that that ensures the continued reign of the Other, the reign of the bourgeoisie. There is still a trace of Sartre's pessimism here because, for him, the series is the archetype of sociality. It is, if we can put it this way, the ordinary structure of the life of the masses.

The emergence of the fused group, which reacts against social inertia, signals, on the other hand, a bid for optimism. It has to be said that there is a certain dialectical obscurity about this. How can men who have been passively brought together in their impotence and separation by large social collectives suddenly call into being an active unity in which they recognize one another? It is worth noting that Sartre, borrowing an expression from Malraux, calls this event an apocalypse. The apocalypse means that the series dissolves into a fused group. The mediation this requires is itself partly external: it is the awareness of its intolerable nature that dissolves the series and creates a new reciprocity. If, for example, the bus we are waiting for in passive indifference does not come along, there will be protests and mutterings. People will start to talk to each other about the inhumanity of their external conditioning. Even at this stage, an element of fusion is already apparent. Unity in separation is practised as an internalized unity: I speak to the Other because he, like me, finds the wait intolerable. What was 'I am the same as the Other whilst being other than me' becomes 'the other is the same as me, and I am no longer my other'. As Sartre says, in the series, unity is created elsewhere, namely in the object. It is a passive unity. In the fused group, the unity is immediately there, within me and in all the others. It is an active unity and a ubiquitous unity. In the series, the Other is everywhere; in the fused group, the Same is everywhere.

It is the ability of everyone to indicate to everyone else their practical unity with everyone else that manifests this new unity. If, for example, someone says 'Let's all protest together', everyone follows his lead because that practical call mediates between each and every one of them. The series really has been dissolved. The person who said that has no institutional or external status. He is the anonymous individual through whom everyone is a possible mediator of the reciprocity of all. He is what Sartre calls the regulatory third party. The regulatory third party is the statute [*statut*] of anyone who has a practical relationship with the reciprocity of all individual praxes. A fused group is made up of individuals who all, in their turn, become the third party who totalizes the interiority of the fused group in action. The third party is neither a chief nor a leader; anyone whose spontaneous indications and directives make it possible for others to dissolve the inertia of the series is a third party. Everyone is a means for the third party to the extent that the third party is the means for the group.

Sartre applies this schema in brilliant analyses of days of rioting or insurrection. He demonstrates the specific workings of serial collectives (the storming of the Bastille). He shows how the intolerable (poverty, fear) brings pressure to bear on inertia. He shows the emergence of fusion (the cry: 'To the Bastille'). But he does so – and this is worth noting – within the framework of bourgeois revolutions, and especially that of 1789. He refers, that is, to days of rioting in which there is no dialectic with institutional political forces, and in which no people's party is present in the masses. From that point of view, fusion is a historico-revolutionary concept, and not a political concept.

The discussion of the third type of gathering – the organization – does deal with politics. The matrix of the organization, or the thing that allows it to move from fusion to institution (which is another serial collective), is the oath. The oath appears at the point where the possibility that the group might disperse has been internalized. As everyone is the third party for everyone else, he fears the dispersed solitude that is both the others' doing and his own doing. It is not enough for reciprocity to be immediate. It requires a stable mediation. It is the oath that allows everyone to commit themselves to remaining the same. The oath gives me a guarantee that the third party will not become the Other; at the same time, I guarantee that I will not become the Other for my third parties. Whatever form it may take, the oath is in fact the group's internal struggle against the imminence of betrayal. Treason is an inevitable threat because separation is the normal form of sociality. If the series is not to reappear, the group must bring a counter-pressure to bear upon itself in the shape of an essential subjective element. That element is fear of the traitor, within others, but also within me.

That the basis of the organizational process is fear, fear of betrayal, reveals Sartre's pessimism. The oath is necessarily supported by an atmosphere of terror. Why? Because no one knows whether the other really is afraid enough of being betrayed. In order to equalize the fear, the group must establish a terroristic reciprocity within itself: anyone who betrays the oath will be punished by everyone else. That is the group's new interiority. Optimism is the terror that goes hand in hand with the advent of fraternity. Given that the group decides its own fate through the oath, everyone is aware of being his own son, and everyone is bound to everyone else by the obligation to supply mutual help. Fraternity is the mode in which everyone experiences, with respect to others, his own birth as an ordinary individual within the group.

The life of the group that is bound by an oath is governed by fraternity-terror. That allows the group to establish the dialectic between practical freedom and the serial; one determines fraternity, whilst the other, which has been internalized by fear, determines the necessary internal oppression of each by all. On this basis, Sartre studies the process that allows us to understand organizations, and then institutions. At each stage, the inertia increases and the memory of fusion fades. Oppression outweighs fraternity. The permanent division of tasks replaces the function of the third-party regulator. The institution brings us back to our starting point: it is a serial collective, and its unity is nothing more than unity in separation. The supreme institution is the state.

Perhaps the most interesting thing about this bonding is the way it allows us to breathe new life into the Marxist concept of class. From 1955 onwards, Sartre fought vigorously against a purely objective or purely social definition of class. In his view, a class was a mobile ensemble articulated into series, groups and institutions. At the level of production, the purely objective reality of the working class is a unity in separation, a passive, serial unity. It is governed by the law of division and competition. All working-class resistance or any shop-floor revolt is a local fusion of a series. Even at that level, we have a principle of subjective reciprocity. Sartre analyses it in detail. Discussing go-slows, he demonstrates that they are a sort of dialectical ethics based upon a rejection of serial competition: 'If a worker says, "I shall avoid doing more than the Others, in order not to require the Others to do more than they can, and in order that I shall not be required to do more than I can by another", he is already a master of dialectical humanism.'[2]

If we think of the great working-class slogans of the post-'68 period in France or Italy, such as 'work at your own pace', we have to pay tribute to Sartre for having noticed that they have important implications for politics, but also, as he rightly says, for ethics.

A class is therefore a series: that is its social being. A class is in fusion: that is its practical being as a mass. A class is an organization: it works upon itself in the modality of terror-fraternity, which is to a greater or less extent stable and which can take the form of a para-state organization like the big unions. And its concrete history, as historical subjectivity, is the

2   Jean-Paul Sartre, *Critique of Dialectical Reason I: Theory of Practical Ensembles*, trans. Alan Sheridan-Smith, ed. Jonathan Rée, London: Verso, 2004, p. 803.

articulated movement of those three dimensions, and never the linear development of one of them. To that extent, Sartre anticipates the necessary distinction between class as social being, and class as historical and political being. Within concrete History, a class exists in the atomized form of the social series, dissolves the series in its revolts, and structures the subject of the revolt against betrayal, or through what Sartre calls the dictatorship of freedom, meaning the fraternal group. It then gives birth to organizations which have a 'dispassionate' capacity for fusion, and they finally revert to being institutions that generate a new type of serial: an institutional division that in a sense replicated division through labour.

All these forms of existence coexist and upset one another in the course of a History that is open. The existence of a class fluctuates between seriality and institutions. That is its organic life. We can, however, identify active, or totalizing, forms of circularity: individual praxis on the one hand, and the fused group on the other. We can also identify passive or totalized forms: the series on the one hand, and the institution on the other. In philosophical terms, this means that the movement of history is not homogeneous and is not the product of unitary dialectic. There are moments that are anti-dialectical moments: that of pure matter on the one hand, as opposed to individual praxis. That of the institution, as opposed to the insurrectionary group. Unlike Hegel, Sartre therefore tries to conceptualize a dialectical continuity. Practical freedom is constantly being turned against itself by natural and institutional inertia, even though material products and institutions are products of praxis. The transparency of the free man is absorbed into its opposite, and Sartre calls that opposite the practico-inert. As a result freedom can only perceive itself at very specific moments: that of the dissolution of the series and that of unifying revolt.

This is undeniably the stumbling block for Sartre's logic. If man is truly human – or in other words capable of reciprocity towards the Other – only during the revolt that dissolves the series, then human unity can exist only in the form of antagonism and violence. The only form of collective activity is the mass movement against social inertia, but that inertia is protected by the adversary and the supreme institution of the state. Passivity is the normal form of sociality. Is history oriented towards a greater liquidation of passivity? That is the meaning of the communist idea. But according to Sartre, serial passivity is a precondition for collective activity. Indeed, men are men only when the series is dissolved. Activity and reciprocity have as their content the destruction of passivity. If the social basis of passivity is restricted, then what existence lies in store for men? According to Sartre, the human is nothing more than the dissolution of the inhuman. The dialectic is conditioned by the anti-dialectic. How can we hope for its stable, or even expanded, advent? One has in fact the feeling that man exists only in flashes, in a savage discontinuity that is, ultimately, always absorbed into inertia and the law of separation. Collective action is the pure moment of revolt. Everything else is an expression of man's inevitable inhumanity, which is passivity.

It follows that Sartre's politics is a politics of the mass movement, which means that it is in many respects an infra-politics. It is typical that, when he examines the question of working-class organizations, it is the trade union that serves as an example, rather as though the logic of trade unions was, in his view, the same as that of political parties. Basically, the Subject that Sartre wants to restore to Marxism is a historical subject. It is, if we can put it this way, a mass-subject. The *Critique of*

Dialectical Reason develops a formidable formal logic
to make intelligible the principle that 'It is the masses
who make History.' What is being conceptualized here
is in a sense the historical know-how of the masses.
But whilst the masses make history, can they, by the
same criteria 'make' politics in the same sense?

Sartre clearly believes that the organization is the
absolute term of politics and that, from that point of
view, we cannot identify History with politics. But
he always looks to the masses in order to discover
the truly dialectical reason of organizations. In his
view, an organization is basically a revolt that has
crystallized. It has crystallized because it has been
forced to internalize the passivity against which the
group rebelled. For Sartre, the political party is still
an instrument. It is instrumental passivity in action.

In my own view, the logic of the political Subject
or the logic of class do not exist in a continuum with
the mass movement. The party is a specific process
internal to the masses, but it brings about a particular
break: the break known as politics, as communism.
The party is therefore something more than an
instrument and something other than an instrument.
The party integrates homogeneous contributions into

its presence within the masses, and they are mainly of an ideological and theoretical nature. The logic of its development is not inscribed solely within the discontinuity of riots. It has a particular continuity, and it is no longer that of the inertia of the institution, but that of the continuity of proletarian politics. And if we are to think the continuity of that politics through to the end, we must take the view that there is more to the masses than the destructive ability to dissolve the series. We have to conclude that mass activity and mass ideas have an internal correctness [*justesse*] that is simply not there in the fused group. In a word, we have to conclude that, at any given moment, popular ideas and practices are divisible and contradictory, and that collective experience is never simply trapped into the activity/passivity contradiction. We can trust the masses precisely because their ideas also have to do with processes that shift their ground and assert something new that exists outside the activity/passivity contradiction.

Ultimately, Sartre fuses politics and History because history's sole driving force is the contradiction between transparent individual practice and inert matter. He draws what conclusions he can from that, and many of them are fascinating. But we can also understand why, after '68, he became the Gauche prolétarienne's fellow traveller.[3] The Gauche prolétarienne had only one slogan: *'On a raison de se révolter'* ['It is right to rebel!']. The *Critique of Dialectical Reason* supplies the reason why it is right to rebel [*'la raison de cette raison'*].

In my own view, the political Subject, which Marxism really does have to theorize anew, never coincides with the subject-in-revolt, even though it presupposes its existence. The fact that the proletariat is active amongst the people is not to be confused with the fact that it is the masses who make History, which is always true. There is within the political subject, and within the process of a new type of political party, a principle of consistency, and it is neither seriality, fusion, the oath nor the institution. It is an irreducible that escapes Sartre's totalization of practical ensembles. It is a principle that is no longer based upon individual praxis.

3   Editorial note: founded in the aftermath of May '68, the Gauche prolétarienne [Proletarian Left] was the largest and most active of France's Maoist organizations. It dissolved itself in 1973.

There are two Maoist realities whose necessity cannot be demonstrated by Sartre. First, trust in the masses, defined as a permanent principle that refers not only to insurgent violence but also to the communist future. Second, the new-style party, which is the support not only for the revolutionary idea but also for a logic of popular unity that is valid in itself: it is affirmative and creative, and not simply warlike or dissolving.

Sartre still remains one of those who re-awakened Marxism. He urges us to reflect upon politics and History precisely because he develops a purely historical and revolutionary conception of Marxism as far as it can be developed. And we need something political and communist [*du politique et du communiste*] as well as the historical and the revolutionary. Sartre invites us to look again at the question of the political subject, and to trace the path for a dialectical-materialist philosophy centred on that question. That is why Sartre is not just a great fellow traveller when we act. He is also a great fellow traveller when we think.

Jean Hyppolite (1907–1968)[*]

In order to do him full justice, we really have to talk about the character of Jean Hyppolite and about his existential singularity, despite the novelty and consistency of what he has bequeathed us. Why is that important? Because Hyppolite established a sort of mediation, which was both quite unusual, and as it happens extremely fragile, between the academic regime of philosophy, within which he worked and held an important position, and what lies outside it. He was, from that point of view,

* Jean Hyppolite directed the Ecole normale supérieure, and was professor at the Collège de France. He was the author of numerous books and translator of Hegel's *Phenomenology of Spirit*. Among his works were *Studies on Marx and Hegel* [*Etudes sur Marx et Hegel*], London: Heinemann, 1969; *Genesis and Structure of Hegel's Phenomenology of Spirit* [*Genèse et structure de la Phénoménologie de l'esprit*], Evanston: Northwestern University Press, 1979; *Introduction à la philosophie de l'histoire de Hegel* and *Logic and Existence* [*Logique et Existence*], Albany, NY: State University of New York Press, 1997.

an exception within the academic apparatus of French philosophy. He defined a singular moment, a sort of bright interval into which we – 'we' meaning those of us who were about twenty around the 1960s – had the good luck to stumble. In those years, thanks to Hyppolite, the bolts on academic philosophy, which were normally shut tight, were released. As a result, he won the support and complicity of Canguilhem, and the two of them became an outward-looking intra-academic duo who accepted what might be called 'the lesson from outside'. That openness had a major impact on a whole sequence in the history of philosophy in this country. Frédéric Worms likes to call it the 'philosophical moment of the 1960s', and it occurred somewhere between 1950 and 1980. That is why the personality of Hyppolite is important. And that is why I ask your permission to be absolutely anecdotal and completely superficial today.

As has already been said in very dense terms, Hyppolite mounted a fundamental operation around Hegel. But there were also a lot of derivative or secondary operations, and they are not all reducible to his plan for a new French appropriation of Hegel that implied a revision of Victor Cousin's old verdict. I would like to devote a few vignettes to those operations.

To turn, first of all, to the translation of the *Phenomenology of Mind* and the never-ending commentary thereon, that defines Hyppolite as a *passeur*, to use the title of today's gathering. In what sense was he a *passeur*, the sort of smuggler who gets people across borders? I was struck by a comment made by one of my German translators, Jürgen Brankel, a philosopher from Hamburg. He told me that he was much more fascinated by Jean Hyppolite's French translation than by Hegel's original book! He took the view that, in German, the book was a typical piece of juvenilia, pretty shapeless, muddled, and that Hyppolite had turned it into a real monument that was completely new. According to Brankel, this 'translation' was in fact a book in its own right, and German philosophy would do well to learn from it. This 'translation' served as a perfect example of what excellent French philosophy is, and demonstrated that Germans should learn from that philosophy, and should by no means take back the book as though it was their property.

It seems, therefore, that *passeur* has to be understood in a very complex sense. Hyppolite apparently got the *Phenomenology* back to the Germans in the form of a book that was originally written in French! We have here a particularly extreme example of what Hegel calls 'extraneation', or the radical effect of mediation through alterity.

It is no doubt that which explains the very particular style of the translation. Let us move to the anecdotal level. When we were young, rumour had it that Hyppolite's German was very poor, and that his translation was a philosophical operation in which the languages in question were the servants of the translator, and not the driving force behind the translation. Someone said this morning that Hyppolite helped to construct a French Hegel, and that in that sense he was the heir to Villiers de l'Isle Adam or Mallarmé rather than the University, even though the latter is an important agent in the history of philosophy. We have heard a striking eye-witness account today, and it defines my early relationship with Hyppolite. For I read and studied that translation for a long time without making any reference to the German text. Fortunately, I was told much later by Jürgen Brankel, that that was the right way to go about it, and that the important thing was to read Hegel only in French.

My second encounter with Jean Hyppolite was
during the entrance examination to the Ecole normale
supérieure. He examined me in philosophy. He had
a slight lisp, and imitating the way he spoke was
a common pastime for *normaliens*. He asked me:
'Monsieur Badiou, what is a thing [*chose*]?', which
he pronounced '*ssoze*'. I gave him my answer. I am
still trying to answer that question in big books: you
never get over your exams. I quickly established a
complicity with him because, in the course of the kind
of rhetorical exercise in which we had been trained, I
cited Parmenides' poem in Beaufret's translation. An
isolated sentence in which Parmenides speaks of the
moon, which I used to describe how far we are away
from the Thing. '*Claire dans la nuit, autour de la terre
errante, lumière d'ailleurs*' ['Night-shining, wandering
about the earth, another's light'].[1] My clever reference
to a light from elsewhere made Hyppolite's face light
up. I was sure I was in a good position now. Even so,
he asked me: 'But what is the real difference between
a *ssoze* and an *obzet* [*objet*/object]?' I improvised an

1   Translator's note: 'Bright in the night, wandering about the
world, a light from elsewhere.' In Jonathan Barnes, ed., *Early
Greek Philosophy*, London: Penguin, 2001, p. 88.

answer. And I have to say that, having worked in recent years, and with great difficulty, on the notion of an object, I still bear that warning in mind. I fear that, even today, I still confuse the two. At that time, having met Hyppolite the *passeur*, I encountered the *organizer* of the philosophical field, an organizer in the sense of someone who can recruit, who knows how to ask the right questions and who can forge alliances, even with people who are far removed from him. I had immediately seen the organizer function in the way he spoke to me.

I subsequently attended his seminar at ENS. It was on Fichte. This was in 1957. He wanted to get Fichte across in the same way that he had got Hegel across. But he sensed that it was not working as well. On several occasions, he said to me 'They like Fichte less than they do Hegel', including me in an objectivized collective. I remember a whole seminar that was devoted to a discussion of contemporary cosmologies, and Hyppolite, with his eternal cigarette holder – you could always see smoke rising over his head, whatever the circumstances – displayed extraordinary knowledge and virtuosity by explaining how the cycle of hydrogen and helium burned. During this inspired

speech, with the blue smoke rising up in the great
tradition of German philosophies of nature, you could
literally see the entire cosmos bursting into flames.
Despite all that, we did not like Fichte. Hyppolite
quickly gave up, concluding that he had failed in
his attempt to interest us in him. I will now use the
word 'inductor': he was someone who has an inductive
relationship with philosophical categories and others
in the present tense. He was trying to extract from the
present the possibilities opened up by a philosophy or
a philosopher, and he would ratify his judgements and
accept the results of his experiment. He was very much
a man of the present, even and especially when he was
using the history of philosophy as a way of inducting us
into the past of the present.

One famous episode concerns the day Sartre came
to the Ecole normale. There are a number of different
versions of the story in circulation, and we have to let
them circulate because, as Lévi-Strauss has taught us,
that is how mythologies come into being. But I have the
right to give you my own version: I was one of the three
people who arranged for Sartre to come, the others
being Pierre Verstraeten and Emmanuel Terray. We
were with the ones who discussed what he was going

to talk about with Sartre. Hyppolite gave us every encouragement. He recognized something of himself in an operation that consisted in bringing before the students of a dominant institution a typical figure from outside who had, of course, like everyone else, been through the Ecole normale supérieure, but who had had absolutely no academic destiny. Sartre taught philosophy in a *lycée*, and then became a *freelance*[2] philosopher. This was where Hyppolite's 'mediator' side came into its own.

Sartre was in the process of completing his gigantic *Critique of Dialectical Reason.* You have to remember that he thought of constructing it as a symphony in two movements. First, a regressive movement, a 'theory of practical ensembles', a foundational and abstract movement. And then the progressive movement of 'totalization without a totalizer' that would reconstruct the entire rationality of History. Obviously very preoccupied with that second movement, he said to us in that strange voice of his, both nasal and cavernous, 'I could talk to you about Egypt. . .'. We were completely lost for words. We steered him back

2   Translator's note: in English in the original.

to his practical ensembles. So Sartre came, to the same Salles des Actes where we are celebrating Hyppolite's memory today, and there was the quite extraordinary scene of his reunion with Merleau-Ponty. Sartre was as if electrocuted by the almost spectral apparition: they had not seen each other for nearly ten years. After the lecture, Hyppolite, who was always very much at ease in his situation as mediator, took everyone to the café – Sartre and Merleau-Ponty, Canguilhem, Verstraeten, Terray, and yours truly. It was the kind of moment of conviviality over a drink that does not happen very often.

Another vignette. It was to Hyppolite that I gave my first big manuscript, that of *Almagestes*, which was published in 1964, but which I'd completed as early as 1959. He had asked me what I was doing, and I had replied that I was writing a novel. 'Give it to me', he told me. So I gave it to him. You have to know, because he also moved in a world 'outside' philosophy, he attached a very great importance to literature. He was a connoisseur of novels, both new and old, a poetry lover who could cite long passages from Valéry, and had given lectures on Claudel as a very young man. He was quite kind about my manuscript, but added: 'Monsieur Badiou, I think you've put some of my words into the mouth of one of your characters.' It was something he'd said in a student discussion . . . a speech about how well Greek temples fitted in with their sites. And he was right! I'd nicked his speech without realizing what I was doing at the time. He had just come back from Greece, and in an earlier conversation he had told me 'I understand their temples', and had gone on to develop a very brilliant dialectic about them, and I'd passed it on to my character. You can just imagine it! He had read my text with extraordinary attention – a somewhat narcissistic attention, as it happens. For those few lines about Greek temples were no more than a mere detail that was lost in a huge manuscript. He had immediately spotted that detail, and was reminding me in friendly fashion that it was, by rights, his.

He was an astonishing *reader*. The many legends that surrounded him included the rumour that he never slept: never more than three hours, some said. He was always reading, thinking, scribbling . . . When he was giving a lecture, he would very often say that he had been thinking about it all night. He would take out a pile of notes that suggested we were in for a lecture lasting for several hours. And then he never looked at them, and talked about something else.

One of the charming things about these improvisations that resulted from a sleepless night was that he almost always drew on Hegel. Nothing to do with the history of philosophy, but he drew on Hegel as though he always had something to say about immediate situations.

To give an example. His great friend – and mine – Dinah Dreyfus, who was an education inspector, was putting on an exhibition in The Hague, at a university, to show some films she had written and directed. In them, I – and I was very young – talked to the important philosophers of the day, including Hyppolite of course. Hyppolite and I set off on some train or other, taking the reels of film with us. He was very tired. So tired that he almost missed the train, and completely out of breath because we had run to catch our broken-winded coach. He gave a magnificent lecture on Bergson. It was complexly improvised, wandered all over the place and only got back to Bergson after a long digression, rather in the way that the solution comes at the end of a detective story. And then, after my brief introduction, we showed the films. All this was in French, and the

Batavian students did not understand a single word. These were the days of French imperialism, already a little worn out, granted, but still unruffled. Afterwards, we went to a primitive arts museum. And then I saw Hyppolite, the great improviser, lost in speculative meditation about statues from Oceania. His meditation over, he treated me to a sumptuous theory about them. Hegel had come back to life, and he ended by saying: 'They are there, like someone who has always demonstrated that a face is a refusal as well as an offering.' I've often wondered if he was thinking about Levinas. I never asked him. At all events, he wanted to tell me, his only audience: 'That is what Oceanic sculptors, working at a specific point in history, have come to reveal to us today.'

The point is that his relationship with History was a relationship with the present. I had long discussions with him when de Gaulle came to power in 1958. According to him, it was a Bonapartist coup: the support of the army, the man of destiny, guaranteed safety for business milieus, a window dressing of popular support, national rhetoric, and so on. He said to me: 'It's like Napoleon III, but the other way around. Napoleon III started with the authoritarian empire and moved in the direction of liberalism, and de Gaulle will start with liberalism and move in the direction of the authoritarian empire.' For once, he was wrong. De Gaulle was, like Napoleon III, swallowed up by liberalism, by Giscard. The problem is that Hyppolite referred to historical modules, which were rather like Ideas. He practised a fairly systematic historical comparativism, rather as though History was a source of examples. In the same way that he was an improviser, I think he was a sort of historical Platonist. What I mean is that he used History to produce figure-Ideas rather than sequences, developments or futures.

Like all French philosophers, he liked politics, and especially talking about politics with friends, or enemies. To turn to the war in Algeria, I would like to place the emphasis on the *administrator*, in a profound sense, and not just in the sense of management. He was absolutely opposed to the war. Careful! He was by no means a revolutionary; he was a parliamentary progressive. The figure of Mendès-France was more or less his point of reference. And yet, in keeping with his political referents, he wanted the Ecole normale to play a part in the process of shaping public opinion. He thought that one of the Ecole's possible vocations was to intervene, as an institutional site, in the process that would one day lead to negotiations and peace. He therefore had an interventionist conception of the institution. I admire this superior Hegelianism, the idea that the destiny of the institution is not its immobility but its ability to concentrate the historical idea itself. I was involved in the implications of this in two important circumstances.

Hyppolite began by convincing me that, in order to strengthen ENS's symbolic position, we had to put an end to the archaic division between the Ecole normale in the rue d'Ulm and the Ecole normale in Saint-Cloud. Why 'archaic'? Because it was very clear at the time that Ulm was for an upper-class elite, and that Saint-Cloud was for a more or less working-class elite. Hyppolite wanted nothing to do with this subordination of the institution to the objective reality of social classes. He wanted to bring the intellectual elites together in a single institution, regardless of their backgrounds. So he asked me to organize a propaganda campaign in favour of merging the two schools. That propaganda did not last long: the powerful *anciens élèves* lobby spoke out, and we saw the appearance of large posters saying that it would mean the end of the Ecole normale, if not the end of the Republic. Hyppolite and I blew it miserably. Almost forty years after our unhappy attempt, another *directeur* of ENS, Gabriel Ruget, also blew it with the much more modest objective of a merger between ENS (Ulm) and ENS (Cachan). That says it all.

Hyppolite wanted us to take a unitary initiative over the war in Algeria. It was to take the form of an appeal, made by ENS itself, to which people with very different political views would rally and then establish a forum with a view to negotiations over Algeria. Once again, I was my *directeur*'s henchman, and I have a whole file on this, full of fine statements, most of them cautious, from all sorts of people. The process got nowhere. But all this is testimony to Hyppolite's role as administrator, as he saw it.

Does that mean that he wanted reconciliation at all cost? I discovered that he was also a violent character. When I put forward a request, which came from students preparing for the *aggrégation*, to invite Deleuze, who had given a magnificent lecture on *La Nouvelle Héloïse* at the Sorbonne, to come and give a lecture on Proust, Hyppolite replied: 'Out of the question; I do not like that man.' He said it with a glacial virulence that left us speechless. What made this man, who was so even-tempered and so conciliatory, make such a radical exception of Deleuze, and call down what looked very much like a curse on him? I have no hypotheses as to why. On other occasions, I was able to see that Hyppolite was quite capable of bringing things to an abrupt conclusion when the question was, in his view, quite clear and settled. So there was also something of the *judge* about him, with all the mystery that still clings to that function.

To close on a more melancholy note. I saw him during the events of May '68. He was at once impressed, worried and pleased to be caught up in living history. That was his Hegelian love of the contemporary. He fought for the reopening of the Sorbonne, which had been closed and surrounded by the police. He intervened, not at all as someone who had, like me, rallied to the dawn-like rise of leftism, but because he was convinced that things should be left to take their own course. If the World Spirit was at work in clashes with the CRS, it was not our job to hinder it. His comments on all that were made with his usual brilliance, but I also had the feeling that he was not well. I thought he was tired, careworn. At one point, he asked me: 'Do you ever think about death, Monsieur Badiou?' That was strange, because his question had nothing to do with his comments on the events of '68. I said, 'No.' And he said to me, 'You are right not to.' We had moved on from Hegel to Spinoza. When, a few months later, I heard that he was dead, I said to myself that he was a man who was prone to a sort of latent melancholy, which one sensed from time to time. And a man who built his love of the present and his intellectual strength with a sort of peculiar energy that was not easy to maintain. Hence, no doubt, the legendary insomnia and the constant smoking.

Basically, he was a man, a philosopher, who paid a high price to keep the depression at bay and to bequeath us so many treasures. Something prevented him from building what he was capable of building in the conceptual realm. The public role – and it was an infinitely beneficent role – that he agreed to play obviously stopped him from doing so. But so did something more secretive and more mysterious that sheds light on his intense relationship with psychoanalysis. In Lacan's seminar, he spoke with virtuosity and particular commitment about Freud's great text on negation. That was because there was within him a subterranean negativity, a primordial 'no' about which we knew little but which was constantly at work.

We know that Hyppolite was a major figure, but we also know that his works are no measure of his importance. I think he knew that, and that that is why he asked me if I ever thought about death. We have never stopped thinking about his death.

Louis Althusser (1918–1990)

For Louis Althusser, questions of thought had to do with battles, frontlines and the balance of power. The recluse in the rue d'Ulm did not give himself time to meditate, or time to withdraw. There was only time to intervene, and his time was limited, unsettled and hurtling, so to speak, towards an unavoidable precipice. The other time was unlimited but that, alas, was a time of pain.

Because it related to the imperative need for action for which time was running out, the self-image of Althusser's thought used the military categories of advances and retreats, territorial gains, decisive engagements, strategy and tactics.

We have to begin by asking: what, according to Althusser, was philosophy's position within the general getting under way [*appareillage*] of theoretical interventions, within the strategic movements of thought?

It was an important position. The clearest proof is probably that, in Althusser's view, the origins of the great historical failures of the proletariat lay not in the crude balance of power, but in theoretical deviations. That is, it has to be said, a strong indication of what he was about, and it has two implications. First, a political failure has to be explained, not in terms of the strength of the adversary, but always in terms of the weakness of our own project. There is nothing more to be said about that rule of immanence. Second, that weakness is always, in the last analysis, an intellectual weakness. Politics is therefore determined as a figure of intellectuality, and not as an objective logic of powers. One can only subscribe to that rule of subjective independence.

It must, however, be added that, for Althusser, theoretical deviations in politics are, in the last analysis, philosophical deviations. When, in *Lenin and Philosophy*, he gives a list of the categories through which these deviations are theorized – economism, evolutionism, voluntarism, humanism, empiricism, dogmatism, and so on – he adds that: 'Basically, these deviations are *philosophical* deviations, and were denounced as such by the great workers' leaders, starting with Engels and Lenin.'[1]

For Althusser, philosophy is therefore the intellectual site where the ability to put a name to the successes and failures of revolutionary politics is decided, if not the successes and failures themselves. Philosophy is the immanent agency that gives a name to the avatars of politics.

Althusser's strategy was therefore always to determine, in each situation, the philosophical act whereby a nominal space could be delineated for the contemporary, or post-Stalinist, crisis within revolutionary politics. That is what he proposed to do from the 1960s onwards by determining the categories of what he called at the time 'the philosophy of Marx'. The preface to *Reading 'Capital'* has as its title a goal, an orientation, and philosophy is its ideal point. The title is 'From *Capital* to Marx's Philosophy'.

Now it so happens that this strategic orientation will encounter and deal with considerable obstacles,

1   Louis Althusser, 'Lenin and Philosophy', trans. Ben Brewster, in Gregory Elliott, ed., *Philosophy and the Spontaneous Philosophy of the Scientists*, London: Verso 1990, p. 185.

and those obstacles gravitate around the very concept of philosophy. As early as 1966, we observe a shift and, at its centre, a self-criticism, at first latent and then explicit. Althusser, who initially assumed that the autonomy of philosophy was in some sense a given, subjects philosophy to increasingly rigorous conditions, so much so that that site of nomination will eventually be prescribed by the very thing it is meant to be naming. As we shall see, the outcome is the central enigma bequeathed us by the work of Althusser: the almost undecidable nature of the relationship between philosophy and politics.

In 1965, Althusser proposes, to use his own words, to 'read *Capital* as philosophers'.[2] That reading is contrasted with two others: those of the economist and the historian. It will be noted that there is no question here of a political reading of *Capital*. What does his philosophical reading consist in? To read as a philosopher is, he tells us, 'to question the specific object of a specific discourse, and the specific relationship between this discourse and its object'.[3] The categories used here – discourse, object –

2   Louis Althusser and Etienne Balibar, *Reading Capital*, trans. Ben Brewster, London: New Left Books, 1970, p. 14.
3   Ibid., p. 15.

are basically very similar to those of Foucault, to whom Althusser pays tribute in the same text as it happens. The philosophical investigation is of an epistemological nature. Through the mediation of the categories of discourse and object, it proposes to establish that *Capital* is 'the absolute beginning of the history of a science'.

As the argument progresses, however, the objective is defined more broadly. Philosophy, or to be more specific, Marx's philosophy or philosophy after Marx, appears to be in a position to offer, in the great classical tradition, a doctrine of thought. It is, in substance, a matter of substituting 'the question of the *mechanism* of the cognitive appropriation of the real object by means of the object of knowledge' for 'the ideological question of *guarantees* of the possibility of knowledge'.[4]

At this point, two remarks are called for:

- For Althusser, philosophy still exists within the regime of a theory of knowledge. The point is to think the knowledge-effect as such.
- The difference between the philosophy of Marx and received philosophy, which can be said

4   Ibid., p. 56.

to be dominated by ideological questions, is that it thinks, not guarantees of truth, but the mechanisms of the production of knowledge. With a tension that evokes Spinoza from the outset, the philosophical break outlined here takes us from a problematic of the possibility of knowledge to a problematic of the real process of knowledge. Philosophy exists with respect to a singular real: that of knowledge. The fact is that there is such a thing as knowledge, and such is the 'there is' without an origin where philosophy is decided, in the same sense in which Spinoza concludes that we have a true idea. Which means, strictly speaking, that if we do not have a true idea, we will be able neither to find nor to enter into philosophy.

On this basis, it is clear that philosophy, so conceived, exists on the same plane as science. It is virtually the science of the knowledge-effect or, as Althusser will say, the theory of theoretical practice.

What is a practice?

The descriptive framework Althusser outlines for historical existence in general is based upon the multiple, and this is an important insight. This multiple, which is irreducible, is that of practices. Let us say that 'multiple' is the name of practices. Or the name of what I call a situation, once we begin to think it in the order of its multiple deployment. To recognize the primacy of practice is, precisely, to accept that 'all levels of social existence are the site of distinct practices'.[5] There can be no apprehension of social existence under the sign of essence, or the sign of the One. I owe my liking for lists to Althusser, and to Chinese politics. Lists are proof that we have a firm grip on the multiple and the heterogeneous. The list of practices, as proposed in 1965, is instructive: economic practice, political practice, ideological practice, technical practice, and finally, says Althusser, scientific practice, adding in brackets, as though this were no more than another name for it, or an illuminating synonym, 'theoretical practice'.

Scientific (or theoretical): this innocent parenthesis, which aligns 'theoretical' with 'scientific', this minor, transitory punctuation that divides only to unite, is the source of all the subsequent difficulties. For what does this parenthesis welcome into the theoretical,

5   Ibid., p. 58.

alongside the sciences, if not philosophy in person?
The real question is whether philosophy demands a
parenthesis, or is in some sense always in parentheses.
All Althusser's efforts are devoted to repunctuating
philosophy, to removing it from parentheses, but the
blank that is then inscribed in those parentheses
can never be completely erased. A little further
on, he expressly indicates that 'theory', the word in
parentheses, gives us a multiplicity: 'Scientific or
theoretical practice [is] itself divisible into several
branches (the different sciences, mathematics,
philosophy).'[6] So, three main branches. It will be noted
that a distinction is made between mathematics and
the sciences in the strict sense, and that mathematics
is by that very fact situated in the theoretical gap
between the sciences and philosophy. And Althusser
has no qualms about claiming that mathematics and
philosophy represent what he calls 'theory, in its
"purest" forms'. Note the inverted commas and the
affectation of purity.

The kinship between mathematics and philosophy
is paradoxical, as Althusser will later denounce

6   Ibid., p. 59.

formalism as a typically modern deviation within philosophy. He often criticized me for what he called my 'Pythagorism', or what he saw as my excessive interpolation of mathematicity into my philosophical argument. As so often happens to the Master's injunctions when the disciple is stubborn, I simply went on to make things worse for myself. Let us say that, in 1965, the kinship serves as a metaphor for the fact that philosophy, sheltered in a parenthesis, is for Althusser an intellectual site that is homogeneous with the sciences, albeit in a form in which the real object is as absent as it is in pure mathematics.

As we know, Althusser will subsequently make a self-criticism of this whole construct on the grounds that it represents a 'theoreticist' deviation. Does this mean that nothing survives of what, in 1965, he claimed to be specific to philosophy? Far from it, in my view. The seeds of all later developments, which contradict the self-criticism, are indeed in the 1965 preface. From the outset, Althusser synthesizes the claims made in *For Marx*, and recalls that Marx's foundational gesture created two things, and not just one, in a single break. Marx created a new science – the science of History – and a new philosophy – dialectical materialism.

But what are the immediate links between these two dimensions of thought in Marx's break? Althusser describes them thus: 'Marx could not possibly have become Marx except by founding a theory of history and a philosophy of the historical distinction between ideology and science.'[7]

This is the source of all the later problems. For rather than being a positive theory of theoretical practice, philosophy looks like a distinction, divorce or delineation. The whole of Marx's philosophical act is contained with the categories through which it becomes possible to distinguish between science and ideology. Philosophy is already what Althusser will relentlessly define it as, using an expression from Lenin: the ability to draw lines of demarcation within the theoretical. Not so much a section through the theoretical as a severing or division [*sectionnement*]. Not so much a theoretical discipline as an intervention.

But before this seed can germinate, and before he can succeed in situating philosophy somewhere other than in the lists of the theoretical or in the parenthesis of the theoretical, Althusser must undertake some very

7   Ibid., p. 17.

complex operations that impact upon the very idea of philosophy, and even more so upon its supposed autonomy.

Essentially, his programme will now be to extirpate philosophy from the parenthesis of the theoretical, which also means this: ceasing for ever to conceive of philosophy as a theory of knowledge and, by the same criterion, ceasing for ever to conceive of it as a history of knowledge. Neither a theory nor a history of the sciences, philosophy is, all things considered, a practice, and yet it is a-historical. This strange alloy of a practical vocation and a tendential eternity will probably never stabilize, but it does at least tell us this: on this point, the entire development of Althusser's thought is a de-epistemologization of philosophy. And to that extent, and rather than continuing it as so many declarations and commentaries – including his own – would suggest, he sets about destroying the epistemological and historicizing tradition in which French academicism is grounded.

Where the concept of philosophy is concerned, Althusser's tactical operations are primarily operations of hollowing-out, suppression and negation. In what he describes as its theoreticist version, philosophy is classically defined by its domain of objects, or in other words by the theoretical practices whose mechanisms it studies. If philosophy is not a theory of theoretical practices, what new object allows it to be defined? Althusser's answer to that question is radical. For his answer is this: none. Philosophy has no real object. It is not thinking about an object.

The immediate implication of this point is that philosophy has no history, because any history is normed by the objectivity of its process. As it has no relationship with any real object whatsoever, philosophy is such that, strictly speaking, nothing happens within it.

This convocation of nothingness, or of emptiness, is in my view essential. The categories of philosophy are indeed empty from the outset, in that they do not designate any real that they can theorize. And that emptiness is not even the emptiness of being whose infinite deployment is investigated by mathematics. For this emptiness is its only positive counterpart: the emptiness of an act, of an operation. The categories of philosophy are empty because their sole function consists in operating on the basis of and in the direction of practices that are already given and which deal with a raw material that is real and that can be situated in historical terms. This is not to say that philosophy is not a cognitive appropriation of singular objects, but to say, rather, that it is a thought-*act* whose categories function with operational gaps, with intervals that allow it to grasp its objects and to make them real.

That philosophy is of the order of the act and of intervention can be deciphered from its very form. Philosophy does proceed via theses. It is a matter of assertion and neither commentary nor cognitive appropriation. In his 1967 lectures on *Philosophy and the Spontaneous Philosophy of the Scientists*, which were republished in 1974, Althusser announces from the outset that 'Philosophical propositions are Theses.'[8] He unhesitatingly adds that such theses are dogmatic theses, and are always organized into systems. The three dimensions of thesis, dogmatism and system express the profound idea that any philosophy is a *declaration*. The *practical* function of philosophy is to declare that there are limits to the categorial emptiness of the object. As we shall see, the declarative form allows Althusser to inscribe the

8   *Philosophy and the Spontaneous Philosophy*, p. 74.

philosophical act within what we will call political relations. And it is in any case true that 'declaration' is, or must be, a political word.

In Althusser's *dispositif*, the great virtue of the affirmative form of philosophy – the thesis of the thesis – is that it rejects any idea of philosophy as question or questioning. Within philosophy itself, it also distances it from all hermeneutic conceptions of philosophy. This is an extremely precious heritage. The idea of philosophy as questioning and openness always paves the way, as we know, for the return of the religious. I use 'religion' here to describe the axiom according to which a truth is always a prisoner of the arcana of meaning and a matter for interpretation and exegesis. There is an Althusserian brutality to the concept of philosophy that recalls, in that respect, Nietzsche. Philosophy is affirmative and combative, and it is not a captive of the somewhat viscous delights of deferred interpretation. In terms of philosophy, Althusser maintains the presupposition of atheism, just as others, such as Lacan, maintain it in anti-philosophy. That presupposition can be expressed in just one sentence: truths have no meaning. It follows that philosophy is an act and not an interpretation.

Althusser calls this act in the form of a declaration the tracing of a line of demarcation. Philosophy separates, disconnects, delineates. And it does so within the framework of one of its constituent tendencies, namely materialism and idealism. Philosophy has no history, both because, in terms of its act, it is nothing more than emptiness, and because there can be no history of emptiness or nothingness, and because its act of delineation, or the drawing of a line of demarcation, is simply repeated in the light of its eternal options. The primacy of material objectivity for materialism; the primacy of the idea and the subject for idealism. In 1967, Althusser writes: 'Philosophy is that strange theoretical site where nothing really happens, nothing but this repetition of nothing.' And he adds: 'The intervention of each philosophy is precisely the philosophical nothing whose insistence we have established, since a dividing-line actually is nothing; it is not even a line or drawing, but the simple fact of being divided, i.e. the *emptiness of a distance taken*.'[9] And yet, with respect to what and in what external history

9   Ibid., p. 197.

does philosophy trace its line through the act that constitutes it in the absence of any object? For the fact that philosophy had no object and no history by no means implies that it has no effect. There is, Althusser will say, no such thing as a history *of* philosophy, but there is such a thing as a history *in* philosophy. There is a 'history of the displacement of the indefinite repetition of a null trace whose effects are real'.[10] But where is the real of that real effect?

This real once more convenes science. That philosophy might be a science of sciences, or that science might be its object is, of course, out of the question. Althusser puts forward a resolutely anti-positivist thesis: 'Philosophy is not a science. Philosophy is distinct from the sciences. Philosophical categories are distinct from scientific concepts.'[11] It is therefore self-evident that these categories are empty. But philosophy also has a 'privileged relation' to the sciences. That privileged link is what Althusser calls 'nodal point no. 1'.[12] What is the nature of its privilege?

10   Ibid., p. 38.
11   Ibid., p. 187.
12   Ibid., p. 191.

The first point is that the *existence* of the sciences is a precondition for the existence of philosophy. Thesis 24 of the lectures on the spontaneous philosophy of the scientists states: 'The relation between philosophy and the sciences constitutes the *specific* determination of philosophy.' And Althusser suddenly states that *'outside of its relationship to the sciences, philosophy would not exist'*. In terms of philosophy's relationship to the sciences, we move from an object-position – that of 1965 – to a conditional position. That is, in my view, a crucial displacement. Like Althusser, I think that the correct relationship between the existence of philosophy and the existence of the sciences is neither an object relationship, nor a foundational relationship, nor one of critical examination, but a conditional relationship.

But how does philosophy reflect upon its scientific conditions, if not in the mode of an epistemological apprehension? What is philosophy's position in the drawing of a dividing line? We are at a dangerous watershed here. For if the demarcation remains, in the earlier style, a demarcation between science and ideology, that means that science and ideology *revert to the position of being an object for science*. The emptiness of philosophy's categories means that we cannot posit that the philosophical act presupposes that philosophy has 'knowledge' of the essence of science. To put it another way: if philosophy has no object, and if science in particular is not its object, the dividing line that inscribes the act and affect of philosophy cannot be a strict demarcation between science and ideology. The famous 'epistemological break' that divides science from its ideological prehistory therefore cannot, as such, be comprised within the act of philosophy. What then can the structure of that act be, and what is at stake in it?

Althusser in fact gives two answers to this decisive question, the whole problem being whether or not they can be reconciled.

The first elaboration of the difficulty consists in radicalizing the breaking of the link between philosophy and science in an attempt to demonstrate that, ultimately, philosophy relates only to itself, and that its entire real-effect is produced within the intellectual space that is instituted by its categorial emptiness. The dividing line traced by philosophy therefore no longer divides sciences from ideologies, but what Althusser calls *the* scientific from the ideological. Thesis 20 of the lecture on the spontaneous philosophy of the scientists states: 'The primary function of philosophy is to draw a line of demarcation between the ideological of the ideologies on the one hand, and the scientific of the science on the other.'[13] This thesis can, however, be truly understood only in the retroaction of Thesis 23, which states: 'The distinction between the scientific and the ideological is internal to philosophy. It is the result of a philosophical intervention. Philosophy is inseparable from its result, which constitutes the *philosophy-effect*. The philosophy effect is different from the knowledge-effect (produced by the sciences).'[14] This is a very radical thesis of immanence. Philosophy does not inscribe within itself any relationship with the real that is historicized by the sciences and by practical ideologies. Its act is the invention of a line that delineates the scientific and the ideological within philosophy, and not outside it.

The 'invention' theme is, in my opinion, the inevitable result of the hollowing out of the object. Whilst philosophy, being conditional upon the sciences,

13 Ibid., p. 83.
14 Ibid., p. 107.

can obviously still handle the real, it cannot tolerate its conditionality without the invention of a specific and imminent naming of its conditions of existence. Philosophy does not think science, but it does invent and state names for scientificity. It follows that the effects of the line it draws are internal to philosophy itself, and that it is modified as a result. But it so happens that, because it is located within the general field of the practices, its immanent modification has external effects. Its immanent modification and its internal effects have a proximate and causal effect on non-philosophical practices, including science. As Althusser says: 'Philosophy intervenes in reality only by producing results *within itself*. It acts *outside of itself* through the result that it produces *within itself*.' This double theme of immanence and invention, which internalizes the philosophical act of drawing a line, is coherent. But the price that has to be paid is clear: the effects that philosophy has outside itself, its effects on reality, remain completely opaque to philosophy itself. It is, in particular, impossible for philosophy to measure or even simply to think its effects upon science or ideologies, because measuring or thinking those effects would presuppose that science and ideology are characterized as such within philosophy. And the rule of immanence makes that impossible. Philosophy, which invents the categories of the scientific and the ideological, is in no state to think the real effect this delineation has on the sciences or on the ideologies. Philosophy is therefore determined, or conditioned, by real practices to the extent that its effect on those practices is, in its own terms, no more than an empty supposition. What cannot be thought [*l'impossible à penser*] comes within the remit of philosophy, and therefore is real, namely the effect it has on those conditions. And it is in that truly profound sense that the sciences are preconditions for philosophy. Not because of the causal link that Althusser sometimes invokes – somewhat imprudently, as when he claims that philosophy itself is essentially the product, within the theoretical domain, of the combined effects of the class struggle and the effects of scientific practice. But in the sense that philosophy's blind spot consists in its effects upon science and, more generally, the real.

And yet this congenital blindness, this point of impossibility, constitutes, in Althusser's view, an obstacle on a different level, and he attaches a decisive strategic importance to it. That level is the level of the singularity of Marxist, or Marxist-

Leninist, philosophy. Or the break in philosophy introduced by Marx, Lenin and Mao. There is no doubt that for Althusser this break means that, even though it is never fully elaborated, the philosophy of Marx and his successors is radically different from earlier philosophies, and from the idealist philosophies of our day, in that it internalizes the system of its preconditions and effects. Althusser thus adopts the old ideal of self-transparency that a strictly immanent doctrine of philosophy would appear to preclude. In April 1968 – note the date – he argues that the Marxist-Leninist revolution in philosophy consists in rejecting the idealist conception of philosophy (philosophy as 'interpretation of the world') – which, as it always has done, denies that philosophy expresses a class position – and in adopting a proletarian class position in philosophy, or in other words, a materialist position, and in establishing a new, materialist and revolutionary practice of philosophy that has the effect of provoking class divisions in theory. Marxist-Leninist philosophy is therefore the only philosophy that does not deny its class-political conditions of existence and that monitors the effects of the division it introduces, not only within itself, but within the theoretical field in its entirety. It is indisputably a philosophy that has a different – enlightened or enlightening – relationship with both its conditions and its effects. It is a philosophy that has been cured of idealist denegations of its practice, and which therefore escapes the regime of blindness imposed by the immanent doctrine. It is therefore a philosophy whose real point, or point of impossibility, is different.

The difficulty is, however, that, as the massive reference to the class struggle indicates, Althusser's line of investigation into the very concept is completely different here. He discusses the absence of philosophy's object, and therefore the status of the dividing line between the scientific and the ideological, in very different terms.

Basically, the displacement comes down to this: philosophy is determined not only by its scientific conditions of existence, but also by its political conditions of existence. We have not only nodal point 1, or philosophy's relationship with the sciences, but also nodal point 2, or philosophy's relationship with politics. And, Althusser adds: 'Everything revolves around this double relation.'[15] The thesis is therefore as follows: philosophy, which has no object and no history, thinks neither the sciences, nor the class struggle or politics, nor the relationship between the two. Philosophy *represents* – the term is Althusser's – both science in politics and politics in science. Here is the text, and it is very dense and quite enigmatic:

Philosophy is a certain continuation of politics, in a certain domain, *vis-à-vis* a certain reality. Philosophy represents politics in the domain of theory or, to be more precise: with the sciences – and, vice versa, philosophy represents scientificity in politics, with the classes engaged in the class struggle . . . philosophy exists somewhere as a third instance between the two major instances which constitute it as itself an instance: the class struggle and the sciences.[16]

How are we to understand this text? We see, first of all, that the space of philosophy as thought is in some sense opened up by the gap between its conditions

15   Ibid., p. 199.
16   Ibid.

of existence: the sciences and politics. We really are emerging from the parenthesis I mentioned just now, which subsumed both philosophy and the sciences under the theoretical. The operator that releases philosophy from its parenthetic confinement is politics, which goes under the name of class struggle. This brings philosophy closer to an operation that makes its conditions of existence compossible, and that is my own definition. Without taking them as its objects, philosophy will circulate between political prescriptions and the scientific paradigm. The emptiness, with its categories, is supported by an earlier emptiness or a first interval that separates heterogeneous truth-practices. The immanent philosophical effect, such as the drawing of a dividing line between the scientific and the ideological, is therefore dependent upon a class. This prescription takes the form of a *position*. The philosophical act is a declaration, but that declaration attests to or represents a position. The important thing is to see clearly that this position is not philosophical as such. It is a class position. We can therefore argue that the philosophical act is immanent within its result because its object is empty, and that it is also transitive with respect to something other than itself, given that it can always be localized in positional terms. Thanks to this duality of conditions, we have a complex effect: that of a *situated immanence*.

It has to be said that Althusser's montage here is very closely interlinked.

First of all, adjustment of what Althusser calls the 'double relationship' – between philosophy and the sciences, and between philosophy and politics – does not really locate its categories, and no doubt we have to make allowance for circumstances and for the fact that the issue remains unsettled. It is striking that Althusser relies heavily upon themes derived from dialectical idealism, such as representation on the one hand and mediation or 'the third' term on the other. He does not normally do this.

What these categories designate is, in my opinion, the relationship of *torsion* that exists between philosophy and its truth-conditions. There are at least two such conditions: the politics of emancipation, and the sciences. Thinking that relationship is something that can only be done within philosophy, as the philosophical act is, ultimately, *that very torsion*. Philosophy – and this is what Althusser foresaw – states or declares that there are truths, but its ability to say so is conditional upon their existence. The philosophical torsion consists in establishing, under the name of Truth or some other equivalent name, the empty space within which a few truths can be *grasped* in the declarative form of their being, and not in the real form of their process. The claim that 'there are' truths is twofold: the real of their processes is a condition of existence for philosophy, and philosophy's grasp of them declares their being.

Althusser comes closest to this vision of things when he argues that philosophy intervenes politically, in a theoretical form, in both domains: that of political practice and that of scientific practice. Both those domains of intervention belong to philosophy to the extent that philosophy is itself a product of the combined effects of those two practices. So you can see that philosophy's distinguishing feature is that the field of its intervention is the very thing that conditions it. Hence the torsion.

And yet, Althusser further complicates the schema by introducing a second torsion, which is immediately obvious when he posits that philosophy intervenes politically. In his view, politics is therefore not only one of philosophy's truth-conditions: it also establishes the nature of the philosophical act. In the last analysis, philosophical intervention, which was a representation and a mediation between the sciences and politics, becomes a form of politics in itself. The second torsion is introduced because one of philosophy's conditions of existence is politics or class struggle, which also describes what we might call the being of the philosophical act.

We are, it will be recalled, in the vicinity of 1968 and its aftermath. That philosophy is basically political was one of the themes of the day. It is therefore all the more interesting to trace this embarrassing pressure in retrospect, especially if we bear it clearly in mind that the fusion of politics and philosophy, which as Sylvain Lazarus has shown, is inevitably articulated with the dominance of the State, is basically a Stalinist idea.

Althusser was now at the extreme point of the pendulum's arc. In 1965, it will be recalled, philosophy exists on the same plane as science. In 1968, it is a figure of the class struggle; it is, to use his formula, class struggle in theory. To reflect upon Lenin reading Hegel in 1914–15 is not, in Althusser's view, a question of erudition. It is philosophy and, given that philosophy is politics in theory, it is therefore politics.

What is being declared here is that there has been
a decisive break in the symmetry of philosophy's
conditions of existence. Politics now has a very
privileged place in the double-torsion system that
sets apart the thought-act we call philosophy. It has
that privileged position because, quite apart from its
conditional status, it penetrates the determination of
the act.

I have called this break in symmetry and the
determinant privileging of one of philosophy's
conditions a *suture*. Philosophy is sutured when
one of its conditions of existence is assigned to the
determination of the philosophical act of distraint and
declaration. When Althusser argues, for example, that
philosophy intervenes, in a theoretical form, in two
domains: that of political practice and that of scientific
practice, and that those two domains belong to it to
the extent that philosophy itself is a product of the
combined effects of those two practices, he sutures
philosophy to politics. A few years earlier, truth to tell,
he sutured philosophy to science in the parenthesis of
the theoretical. Althusser's creative trajectory unfolds
in a displacement of the suture that does not, ultimately,
succeed in setting free the philosophical act as such

or in preserving its immanence, even though he did, as I have said, more than anyone else to announce its rigour. It was only possible to remove the parenthesis that confined philosophy within an encounter with science by enclosing another parenthesis that makes philosophy a sort of genus of the political. That, no doubt, is the site of the blank that is left between the parentheses, and the formal attraction of that blank is the attraction of the suture. Rapid and violent as they may be, the displacements that Althusser makes the concept of philosophy undergo leave intact that empty place where, when it takes up its abode in it, philosophy is, in a sense, jeopardized by one of its purely descriptive conditions of existence. The trouble with sutures is that they make it difficult to read both their edges: philosophy and the privileged condition.

In philosophical terms, the suture, which invests the philosophical act with a singular determination as to its truth, completes and therefore destroys the categorial void without which philosophy cannot be the site of thought. To use Althusser's terminology, we can say that, when it is sutured to politics, philosophy in fact finds a new object (or objects), even though he explains elsewhere, and very firmly, that philosophy

has no object. In a text that I have already cited, he then
says that philosophy intervenes politically in political
practice and scientific practice. But, as we have
learned from Althusser himself, that is impossible. For
the results of philosophy are strictly immanent, and its
act is the only possible point of access to the practical
internality of those conditions.

In political terms, the suture de-singularizes the
truth-process. To be able to declare that philosophy
is a political intervention, one must have a much
more general and indeterminate concept of politics.
We in fact have to replace it with the rare sequential
existence of what Sylvain Lazarus calls *historical
modes of politics*, as these are philosophy's only real
conditions of existence. We thus have a vision of a
politics that is porous to philosophemes. In Althusser's
dispositif, that is obviously the role that is played by
the crude identification of political practice with the
class struggle. Neither Marx nor Lenin stated that the
class struggle could *in itself* be identified with political
practice. The class struggle is a Historical and State
category, and it is only in very specific circumstances
that it becomes raw material for politics. When it is
used as a support for the suture between philosophy

and politics, the class struggle becomes a mere philosophical category, or one of the names for the categorial void from which it emerges. And that, it has to be agreed, is how philosophical immanence takes its revenge.

But the ultimate difficulty arises, I think, when Althusser repeats that philosophy is a political intervention 'in the form of theory'. What is the role of this formal principle, which appears to make the 'philosophical intervention' different from 'other forms' of politics? And what are these 'other forms'? Do we have to conclude that there is a 'theoretical form' of politics and that it is philosophy, and just what is a 'practical form'? The Parti Communiste Français? The spontaneous movement of those who rebel? The activity of states? This distinction is untenable. The politics of emancipation is in reality a site of thought through and through. It is pointless to see in it a divorce between a practical side and a theoretical side. Its process, like any truth-process, is a thought-process that takes place in conditions that are evental [*évenémentielles*], and in a matter that takes the form of a situation.

Basically, what Althusser failed to fully recognize, and what *we* failed to recognize between 1968 and, let us say, the beginning of the 1980s, is that *all* philosophy's conditions of existence are, in intellectual terms, immanent within it. For there is a law that Althusser sometimes does more than notice, and that he sometimes forgets: it is only possible to think the immanence of the results and effects of philosophy if we think the immanence of all the truth-procedures that condition it, and especially the immanence – Sylvain Lazarus calls it the interiority – of politics.

Althusser outlined, if not developed, almost everything we need to emancipate philosophy from both its academic repetition and the morose idea of its demise. The absence of any object and the emptiness, the invention of categories, declarations and theses, the introduction of conditions, the immanence of effects, systematic rationality, torsion . . . all that remains of lasting value, and it is there in his work. The paradox is that he invented this *dispositif* within the framework of two successive logics, which were its very opposite because they were the logics of suturing. Yet that paradox at least teaches us that politicism offers no escape from theoreticism, and nor, as it happens, does aesthetics or the ethics of the other. We have to un-suture Althusser, and set free the universal import of his invention. The method I propose can be summed up in a few maxims. I will give four of them here.

- Expand the conditions to include all the immanent intellectual spaces that generate disparate truths that exist prior to individual events. Not only the modes of science and politics, but also the arts and the adventures of love.
- See conditions, science, politics, art and love, not as a *dispositif* of knowledge or experience, but as a truth-occurrence. Not as discursive regimes, but as ways of being faithful to events. Althusser rejects the category of truth, which he regards as idealist. He identifies knowledge with truth. This is in fact the real survival, in his work, of the French epistemological tradition, which he actually sets out to destroy. And this is also why this thinker, who is so *solidly situated* in the evental prospects of his time, makes it impossible for philosophy to think events as such.
- Posit that the philosophical act lies in neither the form of representation nor that of mediation. That act is a seizure [*saisie*], and therefore a sudden shock [*saisissement*]. This act indicates to us [*nous saisit de ce que*] that truths do exist.

- Insist upon the subtractive dimension of
  philosophy. The historical ethics of philosophy
  requires it to subtract from itself that which
  clutters it up in order to intervene beyond itself.
  It must constantly repeat that, in the revised
  terms of its statement, it is not and never will be
  a politics, a science, an art or a passion. It is the
  place from whence we can grasp that there are
  truths in politics, in science, in art and in love,
  and that those truths are compossible acts that
  allow philosophy to orient time towards eternity,
  to the extent that eternity is the time in which
  truths are at stake.

These are principles, and I absolutely share one of
Althusser's convictions, which he himself contrasted
with the idea of the end of philosophy, even when it
was couched in Marxist terms. The conviction that the
existence of philosophy is unavoidable.

It must be emphasized that, in the 1960s, which
were so marked by anti-philosophy and so open to the
conjoined themes of global nihilism and the reign of
the human sciences, Althusser was almost the only
one to maintain what is for me still a crucial and
disputed statement. I refer to the statement: 'There

is philosophy'. And indeed: there is philosophy in a rational form. In that sense, he was, unlike Lacan, Foucault or Derrida, who were all anti-philosophers, a philosopher. Yes, he was. Not only did he maintain that there was philosophy; he announced that there always will be. Basically, he believed in *philosophia perennis*.

For he wrote, commenting on the eleventh thesis on Feuerbach – and it is, I think, fitting to conclude with this hope, because it is quite true there are moments when hope is no more than the certainty that something will remain – 'Does this sentence [the twelfth thesis] promise *a new philosophy*? I do not think so. Philosophy will not be suppressed: philosophy will remain philosophy.'[17]

17   *Lenin and Philosophy*, p. 201.

Jean-François Lyotard (1924–1998)

Whenever my thoughts turn to the traces, the writing, or even the body, face or, shall we say, the beauty or seduction of Jean-François Lyotard, I always think of the night; of the night in the sense that it is definitively the order in which daylight gradually becomes unthinkable and in which at the same time there is, in which there must be, the inexpressible trace of what will take place as a figure of morning.

Speaking of *The Differend*,[1] I found this title, which is borrowed from the Latin translations of the Bible: '*Custos, quid noctis?*', 'Watchman, what of the night?' What night is this? The night that has come over, or fallen upon, politics as a genre. This is one of the insistent themes of the book: what has happened to us is the realization that politics is not a discursive genre because it is the multiplicity of genres, the being that

1 Jean-François Lyotard, *The Differend: Phrases in Dispute*, trans. Georges Van Den Abbeele, Minneapolis: University of Minnesota Press, 1988.

is not being, but a series of 'there ares'. Or that politics
is 'one of the names of the being that is not'. That night,
according to Lyotard, is now our site: the realization
that what he devoted his life to, absolutely, for some
fifteen years – and I have devoted many more years
to it – is nothing more than one name for a being that
is not. We could, if we wished, take this to mean that
politics is everything, in the sense of a heterogeneous
dissemination which, because it prevents us from
devoting our lives to it, means that we could just as
easily say: politics is nothing, is no longer anything. Let
us not forget, and let us never forget, that, commenting
in 1986 on his book *Libidinal Economy* (1984), Jean-
François Lyotard speaks of 'the haggard desperation
expressed in it'. And let us also recall the commentary
he gave, in 1973, in *Dérive à partir de Marx et Freud*,
on the word *dérive* ['drift'] itself. A drift that not only
goes against the dialectical logic of the outcome, and
not only against Reason: 'We do not want to destroy
Kapital because it is not rational, but because it is';[2]
and not only against critique: 'We have to drift. And do

2   Jean-François Lyotard, *Dérive à partir de Marx et Freud*,
Paris: Union Générale d'Editions, 1973, pp. 12–13.

a lot more than that. The drift is, by itself, the end of critique.'[3] But at bottom, it is a drift that accompanies, brings about and punctuates, the melancholic drift of capital itself.

Jean-François Lyotard can say – and this is what politics is in so far as it is one of the names of the being that is not – this is the night that watches over a thought:

> What the new generation is bringing to completion is the scepticism of Kapital, its nihilism. There are no things, there are no people, there are no frontiers, there is no knowledge, there are no beliefs, there are no reasons to live/die.[4]

Jean-François Lyotard must have had a brutal encounter with this absence of living/dying, must have traversed it and thought it. And clung to it, whilst probably making an exception for love. But he always gave love an exceptional status, even when his political abnegation was at its most intense. Speaking of himself and his friend Pierre Souyri, he recalls that, for twelve years, '[we] devoted our time and all our capacities for thinking

3 Ibid., p. 15.
4 Ibid., p. 17.

and acting to the sole enterprise of "revolutionary critique and revolutionary orientation" which was that of the group and its journal'. But he adds: 'Nothing else, with the exception of love, seemed to us to be worth a moment's attention during those years.'[5]

'With the exception of love'. The final notes on St Augustine do of course speak to us of the resonance of that exception. But as for everything else, there is almost something of a loss to the monastic, energetic and dense abnegation that goes by the name of revolutionary politics, an entombment, a loss that is all the more extensive in that it gradually takes on the form of a commandment. The imperative spoken by the night, or a certain night. Hence the abrupt statement in the 1989 preface to his texts on Algeria. First, 'everything indicates that Marxism is finished with as a revolutionary perspective (and doubtless every revolutionary perspective is finished with)'.[6]

5   Jean-François Lyotard, 'Afterword: A Memorial of Marxism', trans. Cecile Lindsay, in *Peregrinations: Law, Form, Event*, New York: Columbia Press, 1988, p. 47.
6   Jean-François Lyotard, 'The Name of Algeria', in *Political Writings*, trans. Bill Readings and Kevin Paul Geiman, Minneapolis: University of Minnesota Press, 1993, p. 168.

And, closer to the nocturnal commandment: 'The principle of a radical alternative to capitalist domination . . . *must* be abandoned.'[7] The word 'must', the signifier of the imperative, is italicized in the original.

Lyotard's thought is a long, painful and complex meditation on this duty, which is incumbent upon us, now that he is gone. The duty to come to terms with the night without demeaning ourselves. We can also put it this way: how can we resist without Marxism, without, that is to say, an objective historical subject, and perhaps even, as he writes, 'without any attributable ends'. Where is the place of fidelity to the intractable now, if politics is like a name that has been deserted? What of our drift, now that it is night?

It is in the indescribable that lies on the other side of Kapital's blind and blinding persistence. And ultimately, it goes by the paired names of childhood, intimate intractability, the law and immemorial intractability. But perhaps under a whole list of names that fitted out Jean-François Lyotard's philosophical drift over the last three decades.

7   Ibid., p. 166.

Even the word 'Marxism', whose erasure is one of the night's basic givens and whose dissipation acts, in his thought, as an anti-speculative break, even that word can turn back on itself and name the one who watches over the morning. Speaking of his differend with Pierre Souyri, and in the very course of that differend, Lyotard discovers that, at the very moment when Marxism is a 'vaguely outmoded' discourse, at the moment when certain of our expressions become 'unpronounceable', we stumble across its name and 'something, a distant assertion which escaped not only refutation but also decrepitude, and preserved all its authority over the will and over thought'.[8] He concludes, in what is in my view a decisive passage:

I experience, to my surprise, what in Marxism cannot be objected to and what makes of any reconciliation, even in theory, a deception: that there are several incommensurable genres of discourse in play in society, none of which can transcribe all the others; and nonetheless one of them at least – capital, bureaucracy – imposes its rules on the others. This oppression is the only

8   Lyotard, 'A Memorial', pp. 54–5.

radical one, the one that forbids its victims to bear witness against it. It is not enough to understand it and be its philosopher; one must also destroy it.[9]

The text summarizes everything that allows thought to retain the strength of the morning throughout the night. Allow me to list those supports, or those strokes of luck.

1. First of all – and on this point my agreement with Lyotard is profound, essential – there is the multiple. Uniform and imposed as it may be, night falls only on the heterogeneous and multiplicity. Being is essentially plural. Paragraph 132 of *The Differend*: 'In sum there are events: something happens which is not tautological with what has happened.' Which could be rephrased as: there are singularities. Which gives, in the dispersive form of the question: Is it happening? Well, there are truly proper names. Paragraph 133: 'By *world*, I understand a network of proper names.' The distinctive feature [*le propre*] of proper [*propre*] names is that no one sentence can claim to exhaust their plural.

9   Ibid., p. 72.

2. The oppression is certainly that a discursive genre, Kapital, imposes its rules on others. And because there is no alternative politico-historical subject, just as there is no proletariat, this imposition is in some sense irreversible, or eternal. Kapital is the nocturnal name of the being that is. But the imposition of a rule is nothing more than a surface capture. In ontological terms, the incommensurability of genres of events, the heterogeneousness of what happens, cannot but persist, cannot but insist. The intractable remains intractable, silent under the rule that orders its reduction.

This motif explains why 'Marxism', which was, for Lyotard, the name of politics, remains, can still remain, the economic name for the intractable, or at least one of its names, now that it is void of all politics.

This movement was already outlined in *Dérive à partir de Marx et Freud*. Its purpose, and here I am in complete agreement, was to make a critique of the bureaucratic theme of efficiency. Lyotard advanced the powerful thesis that what had destroyed revolutionary parties and groups was 'the primacy given to transformative action'.[10] Or as I would put

10   *Dérive à partir de Marx et Freud*, p. 19.

it today: politics is not the realm of power, it is the realm of thought. Its goal is not transformation; its goal is the creation of possibilities that could not previously be formulated. It is not deduced from situations, because it must prescribe them.

But what does Lyotard cause to appear against what is still a critical background? What he calls 'another *dispositif*'. And he says of it that it stands, in relation to Kapital, 'in a relationship that is not dialectical, not critical, but compossible'.

That, no doubt, is the central problem of modernism. What is a relationship of negativity? What is a non-dialectical alterity? What is a non-critical compossibility? And, in the background, two paths:

- That of the infinitesimal negative, of the void that has no predicate, of mathematizable and indifferent multiplicity. Here, the relationship is one of pure logical appearance. Politics is preserved in all its diurnal strength because it did not and does not need any alternative subject. 'Proletarian' is the name of disparate and sequential singularities, and not that of a historical force. This is the path that I take, and that Lyotard always criticized as

a deadly identification of descriptive sentences
with normative sentences, or as an inverted
maintenance of the defunct Narrative.

- The other path, which is in theory taken by both
Lyotard and Deleuze, borrows this relationship,
in which there is no negativity or non-dialectical
alterity, from the Bergsonian *dispositif* of life, or
of qualitative duration. For example: 'There is a
perception and a production of words, practices,
and forms that can be revolutionary, but there
is no guarantee that they are sensitive enough
to drift with the great currents, the great *Triebe*,
the major flows that will displace all visible
dispositifs and that will change the very meaning
of operationality.'[11] As we can see, the drift
presupposes the qualitative pressure of flows.

And yet, different as they may be, the axiomatic path
and the vitalist path diverge only at the point where
we have to think the relationship without resorting
to negativity, think the incommensurable without the
transcendence of any measure. The dawn-like feature
of the night, or what thought must take into its care, is,

11   Ibid., p. 16.

then, that there are multiple 'compossibles', but that they are not 'co-thinkable', to use the formula Lyotard applies to what is at stake in the drift.

So, there is the multiple. And there is the incommensurable, and the intractable. Hence the return, at the end of the text I am rearticulating here, of the motif of destruction. 'It is not to understand this oppression and to be its philosopher; one must also destroy it.'

We have to dwell on this point. 'Destroy' is the name for what divides philosophy from what can be demanded because we suffer some wrong or oppression. The 'also destroy' is that which surpasses the philosophical understanding. And if the name for this 'destroy' is no longer 'politics', what is its name or what are its names? Who, in the darkness in which we find ourselves, and which is the obsolescence and erasure of politics, watches over the morning, wearing out and destroying the night? Basically, there is, in Lyotard's view, only one question: what is, where is, *colour*, and where does it stem from?

In order to isolate this question, we must, early in the morning, lose our fondness for the uniformity of the shadows. The conjoined names for that uniformity are Kapital and bureaucracy. Losing our fondness for it implies its destruction. That loss of fondness for it has a long history, both personal and collective, that has been almost forgotten, and yet all Lyotard's thought is its statement, its balance sheet and conceptual statement of account.

Yes, I want to pay tribute, here, to what is, in his language, a *figure*. The Jean-François Lyotard for whom there was nothing more essential than conjoining stubborn and critical thought, radical critique, and organized practice, with the factory as referential link. I want to pay tribute, here, to the Lyotard of Renault-Billancourt because everything stems from that, with, as I have said, the exception of the obligation to love. How many of us are there who spent not a week or even three years, but fifteen years, or even much longer, measuring philosophy by the standards of the vital, thinking intensity of meeting up with a few workers in the early morning? How many of us are there who can speak, freely and loudly in the way that Jean-François Lyotard was still speaking in 1989, of 'the few activists, workers, employees and intellectuals who came together with a view to pursuing the Marxist critique, both theoretical and practical, of reality to its extreme consequences?'

And this is, perhaps, one of the ways to distinguish between what he calls a figure, and what is ubiquitously known as an image.

When Sartre, manipulated by Benny Lévy and the Gauche prolétarienne, climbed on to a barrel outside Renault-Billancourt's gates, it was an image. It was a deliberate ploy to produce an image that could be transmitted and used by the media. It was a publicity stunt. When thought and action are concentrated on the 'factory' site, when there someone watches over the morning, that is a figure, which has no image and which no medium can capture. Lyotard was quite right when he said, without boasting about it, that during those years 'the group respected the asceticism of its own effacement, and allowed the workers to speak'.

That is what I want to salute: that a philosopher's morning can be at a factory; not in the heavy, substantial sense of class, vanguard or the people-in-itself, but, on the contrary, in the sense of the lightness of a trajectory, the obstinacy of a clarity, a drift, a departure, non-dialectical alterity and the non-critical relationship. In the sense of politics as creation and, first and foremost, the creation of improbable places and imperceptible conjunctions.

'To its extreme consequences', said Lyotard. This principle – to its consequences, no matter how extreme they may be in the eyes of current public opinion – is philosophically crucial. To my mind, it is the law of some truth or other. For all truths are woven from extreme consequences. Truth is always extremist.

Jean-François Lyotard had to endure so many breaks, to their extreme consequences. In the background: Trotsky's apparent break with Stalinist terrorism in the 1930s. And then the post-war break with that break because, as he reminds us, Trotskyism could not 'define the class nature of so-called communist societies'. Joining the 'Socialisme ou barbarie' group in 1954. The trouble over the departure of Claude Lefort in 1958. And from the 1960s onwards, the first suspicions about politics as a generic or destinal name for the intractable.

The fact remains that what was done to the proletariat was not 'a particular tort, but a tort in itself'. But the problem that now arises from the profound decomposition of activities and ideals is precisely understanding how the revolutionary project can be expressed and organized, and how it can fight.

A certain idea of politics dies in this society. Certainly, neither the 'democratization of the regime', called for by unemployed politicians, nor the creation of a 'large unified socialist party' (which will only regroup the refuse of the 'left') can give life to this idea. Such notions lack perspective, are minuscule in relation to the real dimensions of the crisis. It is now time for revolutionaries to measure up to the revolution to be made.[12]

Which tells us that it is in not 'being up to it' that the intractable originates.

1964: the great split in the group, with Cornelius Castoriadis on one side, and the 'Pouvoir ouvrier' group, which Lyotard joined, albeit with growing doubts, on the other.

And in 1966, the resignation from 'Pouvoir ouvrier'. And the split with friend and founder Pierre Souyri.

And in 1968, the self-evident truth, for Lyotard, that the proletariat is at best a ponderous *arrière-garde*, that the supposed-subject is amorphous, that history is erratic. The text '*Désirévolution*' says it in poetic terms:

12   Jean-François Lyotard, 'The State and Politics in the France of 1960', in *Political Writings*, p. 276.

But that was the very essence of history the void into
which we threw our stones the absence of a referential
the groping night Violence of the absent meaning a
question dug up from the cobblestones and hurled
beyond all institutions. Negativity is a challenge to
that which represses or represents it. Thanks to its
gesture the pious discourse of the political paradise,
be it today or tomorrow, collapses into vanity. They
did not see that. That what is beginning is not a
crisis leading to another regime or system thanks to a
necessary process. That the desired other cannot be
capitalism's other because the essence of capitalism
is that its other is inside it and can therefore be
recuperated That the other who was openly desired
is and will be desired is the other of the prehistory
in which we are in irons *a scream demeaned to the
status of the written* gin-palace images consoling
music invention banned or patented game broken in
two work and leisure knowledge schized into science
love into sex And society's open eye in its midst the
Greek eye their politics is busy filling it with sand
What has been announced is the beginning of history
the opening of the eye They refuse to see.[13]

13   *Dérive à partir de Marx et Freud*, pp. 34–5.

That allows us to rephrase the question: where is colour? This in the typically matinal question: what is the opening of an eye? A blink, scarcely a flash. A thought: scarcely a cloud. That is what he says. Listen: 'Thoughts are not the fruits of the earth. They are not registered by areas, except out of human commodity. Thoughts are clouds. The periphery of thoughts is . . . immeasurable.'[14] The opening of the eye on to a cloud is a combination of two reversible movements. One is an open/closed blink. The other is a figural displacement. Lyotard will never stop seeking the point of reversibility, which also comes about as a coincidence. At the point where eye opens to see to the most improbable figure of a cloud.

We can also say: thinking is the out-of-tune superimposition of an external different and an internal different. Neither the cloud nor the eye can be reconciled, either with each other or within themselves. The mutation of the figures goes on indefinitely, and the open can never proceed from the closed, even in a negative sense. This is the non-dialectical point we must grasp: blinking,

14   Lyotard, *Peregrinations*, p. 5.

displacement, and finally: the event of the intractable, a blink attuned to a displacement. A miracle. After all, thought is nothing more than a miracle, and that is why, increasingly, Lyotard took the view that the singularity of art was its main repository. Painting, figural, or rather: where the figural struggles against the pictural.

But it has to be said again: the word 'Marxism' itself could name, encore, the non-dialectical point, the reversible. Let us listen to the very end of 'A Memorial for Marxism':

> Marxism is then the critical intelligence of the practice of . . . divisiveness, in both senses: it declares the divisiveness to be found 'outside', in historical reality; the divisiveness 'within' in, as a differend, prevents this declaration from being universally true once and for all. As such, it is not subject to refutation; it is the disposition of the field which makes refutation possible.[15]

A practice that goes in two directions, and therefore a directionless trajectory. This, according to Lyotard, is

15   Lyotard, 'A Memorial', p. 73.

the support the philosopher seeks when he at last loses his fondness for the proletarian Narrative.

And no doubt our differend has to do with the fact that I was more interested than him in the process as opposed to the miracle, in truth as opposed to figures, in mathematics as opposed to language and right, in decisions as opposed to advents, in orientation as opposed to the reversible, in the factory as political site as opposed to the factory as subject of history. Perhaps he would have said that I was pictural, and not figural. A bit too dense, not sufficiently volatile. Still a modern.

For a long time, our relations were extremely irritated. Post-'68 things were violent, coloured, difficult. Lyotard had nothing but contempt for Maoism, which was the virulent inspiration behind our actions. As early as 1958, the 'Socialisme ou barbarie' group published a major article by Souyri entitled: 'The Class Struggle in Bureaucratic China'. Proving, in rigorous terms, that Maoism was a sham was one of the specialities of Lyotard and his friends. That did not make things any easier, believe me. And nor did the little faith he had in one of the key-signifiers in our thought, the 'masses' signifier given in the mass line, mass action and mass democracy. In 1972, he wrote: 'Don't say that we know what the masses desire. No one knows, not even them. Nothing will change if you become the servants of what the masses desire, act in accordance with your supposed knowledge, and lead them.'[16] Yes, there was a political gulf between us. And then, for him, politics withdrew as the privileged site where the intractable manifested itself. For me, it was a truth-procedure that could be sequentially inferred from evental singularities; it was still there, and so was the factory. A certain peace was suddenly possible, and there was what he described in his dedications as an 'affection' between us, though it was distant, smiling and unexplored. Our peasant ancestors, it has to be said, came from the same lost village on the Upper-Loire plateau. It is called Moudeyres. In Moudeyres' cemetery, almost everyone is either a Badiou or a Lyotard, reconciled not so much by death as by the unfathomable density of time.

I would now view our differend in very circumscribed and specific terms, not that that makes it any less serious. Quite the contrary. It is, as always and as with

16   *Dérive à partir de Marx et Freud*, p. 19.

Deleuze, about immanence and transcendence. One crucial utterance, with which Lyotard determines, in *The Differend*, one of philosophy's major requirements is as follows: 'The phrase formulating the general rule for operating the passage from one phrase to the next is itself subject to this form of operating the passage.'[17] Using the Kantian lexicon that he, like all Hegel's enemies, is so fond of, he also rephrases this as: 'the synthesis of the series is also an element belonging to the series'.[18]

Well, no. That is what I do not think. There is a real excess, something with no place, a gap. And if we call it transcendence, too bad. The most banal example is that the series that makes a finite whole number is not a finite whole number; indeed, it is an entity that is truly inaccessible. The immanent principle of that which is repeated or succeeded is neither repeated nor succeeded.

That is probably the whole point that differentiates between us as to what, during the night, should be kept in the future anterior of the morning. The serial logic

17   Lyotard, *The Differend*, p. 60.
18   Ibid.

of the drift on the one hand, the localization of the point of excess on the other. The intractable finitude of childhood on the one hand, and the heightened, faithful projection of the exceptional on the other.

Ultimately, this is a differend about infinity, I think. Or about its correlation with the finite. Which should make it plain that I am both less inimical to Hegel than he is, and also less inclined to make concessions to Kant over the motif of the Law, and that enthusiasm is ultimately, as Lyotard writes, 'an extremely painful joy'.[19]

A differend over the essence of the infinite, but not really about its use. The important point, after all, is to retain the ontological sovereignty of the multiple, and to call it the infinite. In *The Differend*, Lyotard repudiates the notion of Human Rights. Neither 'rights' nor 'human' are appropriate, he quite rightly notes. He also posits, again quite rightly, that 'rights of the other' is not much better. And he finally suggests, in a magnificent expression to which I bow, the 'authority of the infinite'.

There. I would like to end today on this agreement; this philosophical communion beneath the authority

19   Ibid., p. 166.

of the infinite, which requires us to drift and to destroy, which requires something that is not. That is what is required of all thought, but thought is not to meet the requirement. There is what I would call a prior decision. And what he would call an affect. It is written in *The Differend* that 'This is the way in which Marxism has not come to an end, as the feeling of the differend.'[20] Let us say: politics remains, as an excessive decision. And we will have something of an affectionate differend with Jean-François Lyotard over, as Rimbaud would have it, *the place and the formula*.

20   Ibid., p. 171.

Gilles Deleuze (1925–1995)

How is it that, even more so than ten years ago, he is our contemporary? And how is it that he is still out of step with the times, so out of step as to be that rarity: a future contemporary? He is certainly not 'modern' in the eyes of the academics who write the balance sheet of the twentieth century as though its spirit had always resided in the discussion, which now triumphs in our classrooms, between pious phenomenologists and democratic grammarians. Speaking of phenomenology, Eric Alliez is quite right to say that Deleuze's most constant – and most difficult – project was to prove that we can escape it. And that we must do so because it had, as he put it, 'blessed too many things'. As for analytic philosophy and the 'linguistic turn', he hated them with a vengeance, and took the view that a sort of Viennese commando had, at least in university philosophy departments, turned the rich American thought of the Emersons, the Thoreaus and the Jameses into a desert. As for

democracy, it cannot be said too often, given that it is
such a courageous and correct declaration, that one
of the major characteristics of philosophy according to
Deleuze is that it positively loathes the very notion of
'debate'.

But that does not necessarily mean that Deleuze
completed the Heideggerian programme of modernity
– that interminable 'end of metaphysics' that also goes
by the name of the work of deconstruction. He liked to
say that he had no problem with metaphysics. It is not
easy to insert Deleuze into the usual genealogies. Of
course he held that our times began with Nietzsche,
as do so many others, and credited him – though this
is not, in my view, his most powerful inspiration –
with having introduced into philosophy the notion of
meaning, as opposed to that of truth, which had been
killed by conformisms. And yet this Nietzsche, whose
ancestor is a Spinoza baptized the 'Christ of philosophy'
and whose French brother is Bergson, would surprise a
lot of people. Truth to tell, Deleuze constructed a very
unusual history of 'interesting' doctrines ('interesting'
was a word he liked) that was meant only for himself:
the Stoics and Lucretius, Duns Scotus, Spinoza and
Leibniz, Nietzsche, Bergson, Whitehead . . . It is not

easy to generalize this panorama, or to make it the stigma of a shared 'modernity'.

Shall we say, then, that he is, as transatlantic classifications tend to see him, one of the postmodern (or post-postmodern?) representatives of continental, and especially French, thought of the 1960s? If we do, we forget that, at the time, he was swimming against the current. He spoke very eloquently about structuralism, about non-meaning as the cause of meaning, and about the theory of the 'empty set'. He shared certain of Blanchot's analyses of death and writing, but he also rectified them. But he did not belong to that school, and still less does he belong to it ten years later. His polemic against Lacan was violent, and he challenged him – in vain – with his schizoanalysis. His 'Marxism', fraternally woven together with Guattari, was the complete antithesis of Althusser's. Which leaves, obviously, the deep friendship that governs his tributes to Foucault. Although I do not have time to prove it here, I insist that their creative friendship must not conceal the fact that it changes completely as their central idea of what a concrete singularity itself is changes.

So how can we evoke him for our times? Why is it so obvious that he is by our side, even in the ironic distance of his perpetual retreat from the frontline where we were fighting against reactive infamy? I will disseminate this evidence in five major motifs, which are all bound up with the realization that something has been exhausted (another word he liked). He was often 'exhausted', and felt at such times that he was a brother to many of his heroes, such as Melville or Beckett.

1. Deleuze contrasted all thought of 'ends' (the end of metaphysics, the end of ideologies, the end of grand narratives, the end of revolutions . . .) with the conviction that nothing was 'interesting' unless it was affirmative. Critique, impotencies, ends, modesties . . . none of that is as valuable as a single real affirmation.

2. The motifs of unity, gatherings, 'consensus' and shared values are nothing more than thought's tiresome moment of fatigue. What does have value is certainly synthetic, as is all creativity, but in the form of separation, disjunction. Disjunctive synthesis: that is the real operation of anyone who is 'forced' to think (for we do not think 'freely', we think under pressure, we think as 'spiritual automata').

3. We have to stop speculating about time, its precariousness, and its subjective ubiquity. For what

matters is eternity or, to be more specific, the temporal atemporality that has received the name 'event'. The great and unique 'throw of the dice' on which life wagers both its chance occurrence and its eternal return.

4. We have to get away from the obsession with language. Speech is of vital importance, but it is caught up in its multiform correlation with the integrality of affirmative experience, and has no constituent syntactic power. To confuse philosophy with grammar or with an inventory of rules is aberrational. Let us abandon, like an old corpse, the idea that the natural form of thought is judgement. And above all, do not judge: that is a good axiom for thought. Replace judgement with personal experience, with becoming 'caught up in our milieu'.

5. The dialectic is exhausted. We must rise up against the negative. In accordance with the 'Return' method, this brings us back to point 1: finding the integral affirmation of the improbable and doing so ascetically, which means of course without any negation of any kind, trusting – involuntarily – in becomings.

I would happily say that what sums up all these precious lessons – both for him and for me, even though

I agree with neither the details nor the argument – can be summed up in one negative prescription: fight the spirit of finitude, fight the false innocence, the morality of defeat and resignation implicit in the word 'finitude' and tiresome 'modest' proclamations about the finite destiny of the human creature; and in one affirmative prescription: trust only in the infinite. For Deleuze, the concept is the trajectory of its real components 'at infinite speed'. And thought is nothing more than a burning to a chaotic infinity, to the 'Chaosmos'. Yes, that is the frontline I was talking about earlier, the frontline where he stands alongside us, and by doing so proves himself to be a very important contemporary: let thought be faithful to the infinity on which it depends. Let it concede nothing to the hateful spirit of finitude. In the one life we have been granted, and caring nothing for the limits that conformism assigns us, we will attempt at all cost to live, as the Ancients used to say, 'as immortals'. Which means: exposing within us, so far as we can, the human animal to that which exceeds it.

Michel Foucault (1926–1984)

A philosopher, on the edge of a mutation in thought, its objects and its ends. And who attempted to capture, against the background of a Nietzschean genealogy, the configuration wherein it becomes meaningful to say that there is at, at some point, some truth-gesture.

An intellectual – and opposed, he used to say, to those who are sickened by the word.

A solitary figure of mastery, with no school, with no one around him, and often silent.

A scholar, in the excellence of that term, full of humour, modest and capable, when necessary, of great rational violence.

Someone whose invisible master was always Georges Canguilhem. In whom we can recognize the same taste for hard work, documented proof, for interruptions, and for such occasional certainty that never failing to observe it was an ethical rule.

A written French that was at once rapid and cursive, quick to evoke images, and just as quick to revoke them.

Letters of nobility that were above all suspicion conferred upon the library, on collation, on the archive.

The capacity to surprise, and also the ability to disappear. A radical lack of ostentation, a man of the métro and the crowds who taught the few, anonymous glory hiding behind a proper name.

An activist who supported individual causes – all causes are individual – a man for the streets and for declarations. The ever-admissible alliance of the majesty of the chair and the banality of prisons.

In short, and whether we read him, read little of him, agree with him or disagree, a barrier against vulgarity in these debased times. There are not many such men left, either in knowledge or in the institutions. Which leaves us a little more exposed, a little more vulnerable.

For a generation of philosophers, the danger was the war, the Resistance. We lost Cavaillès and Lautman to them. For Foucault, the danger was simply the world as it is, without grace, and in the asphyxia, which always begins anew, of anything with claims on the universal.

He – this benefactor – was on the same level as the world. Personally, I now feel with a penetrating disquiet that he was a sort of distant but reliable dyke against everything in the world that is base and irrevocably submissive. He was concerned to know that a subject can have a legitimate relationship with himself. And so, in keeping with an essential national tendency, the finest dispositions of knowledge were subordinate to ethics.

We have to speak of Foucault's rationalism, and indicate its tensions and extent. And add that having faith in the detail of his constructs is not as decisive as accepting that there can be no compromise over the ambition and universality of the *dispositifs* of knowledge.

The latent discussion of 'What is a modern intellectual?' is no grounds for replacing Foucault with a non-existent Foucault on the pretext that he is dead. What sense is there in recruiting him into the limited earnestness of specialists, into Mitterrand's ministries or the junk of journalism?

As for contrasting him with Sartre, that is a scholastic exercise.

Of course we all broke with phenomenology, the theory of consciousness and the last avatars of psychologism, and he had not a little to do with that. Foucault gambled what Canguilhem confined to the strictly circumscribed domains of science or medicine on what we thought came within the remit

of the human sciences, history or anthropology. The
clinic, madness, money, linguistics, botany, the
penal system, sexuality . . . But this was neither
history, anthropology nor the human sciences.
It was a gesture that annexed for philosophy, for
pure thought, objects and texts that had been
divorced from it. We occupied the territories of that
annexation, even when Foucault's gesture seems to
us to be incomplete, or difficult to follow.

But with hindsight, it will become clearer that he
embodies a fidelity – all true fidelity is a break – to
the defining characteristic of French intellectuals.
It is the heritage of the eighteenth century, and it
means that they are at once critical rationalists,
political witnesses, people with a polymorphous
curiosity, and writers. Before Foucault, Sartre was
the modern name for that heritage. The justice of
the times was to bring Sartre and Foucault together
in the Goutte d'Or area of Paris to protest about
the murder and expulsion of immigrant workers.
Nothing can prevail against that photograph.

I rarely met him in recent years, except at the theatre.
That is, after all, the right place for such encounters. We
go there to go on with the delectable process of losing

our fondness for any representation or performance [*représentation*]. That is what plays now purge us of. Foucault knew full well that, where that is concerned, literature is our escort; witness his reading of Raymond Roussel, witness the critic he could have been.

Let no one try to tell us that, after that, the question of commitment and its general value has disappeared along with Foucault. Even Foucault's apparent mistakes teach us the opposite. His statement on Iran, and he was made to pay a high price for it, was testimony to his appetite to go on reading into history the advent of a different regime of collective truth.

Despite what one read here and there, it was indeed the universal that made him so self-assured, and what he had to transmit is very relevant to what we must do to change both ourselves and the world.

The tribute we should pay to Foucault is now to read his last book, to talk about it with exactly the same rigour as though he were alive.

I am already personally moved, touched, that, speaking of his attempt to trace the Graeco-Roman genealogy of the mastery of sexuality, Foucault reintroduces the category of the Subject, and especially that he states (in the interview published in *Les Nouvelles* on 29 May 1984): 'I will call the process whereby we obtain the constitution of a subject Subjectivation.'

For the only conformism one could detect in Foucault – a conformism established and maintained by almost all recognized French philosophers – was that, at least in his theoretical writings, he tried to avoid Lacan.

For his sole concern was with what was vouched for by his inner, abrupt and laughing conviction, and that conviction was both tenacious and armed with science.

Jacques Derrida (1930–2004)

There was in France a philosophical moment of the 1960s, to use an expression dear to Frédéric Worms. Even those who have apparently tried to organize its forgetting know that. Not much more, perhaps, than those five intense years between 1962 and 1968, between the end of the war in Algeria and the revolutionary storm of the period 1968–1976. Just a moment, yes, but it really felt like a moment of searing intensity. We can say, now that Jacques Derrida is dead, that the philosophical generation which identified that moment is almost completely gone. Only one retired tutelary figure remains, an old man who is impassive and covered in glory: Claude Lévi-Strauss is the only one left.

The first feeling I experience is therefore not a very noble sentiment. I actually said to myself: 'We are the old ones now.'

So, we ... We ... who are we? Well, to be quite specific, it means we who were the immediate disciples of those who have passed away. We who were aged between twenty and thirty in those years from 1962 to 1968, we who followed the lessons of those masters with passion, we who, as they grew old and died, have become the old ones. Not in the same sense that they were the old ones, because they were the signature of the moment of which I speak, and because the present moment probably does not deserve any signature. But we are the old ones who spent our entire youth listening to and reading such masters, and discussing their propositions day and night. We once lived in their shelter, despite everything. We were under their spiritual protection. They can no longer offer us that. We are no longer divorced from the real by the greatness of their voices.

I therefore insist – I feel that duty demands it – on paying tribute to Jacques Derrida, who has died so suddenly, and, in doing so, paying tribute to all of them. To all the dead signatories to the great moment of the 1960s.

A philosophical tribute is what I believe to be the fitting tribute. A tribute that signals the gap and gives it a power of its own. In order to pay that tribute, I need a few preliminaries, and I will here give them an extremely simple form.

A justified simplicity. For there was, beneath the astonishingly volatile fluidity of his writing, an authentic simplicity about Derrida, an obstinate and unchanging simplicity. That is one of the many reasons for the violence of the attacks made on him, just after his death, especially in the American press. The attacks on an 'abstruse thinker' and 'incomprehensible writer' were no more than the most banal anti-intellectual insults.

Let us call the insults 'Texan', and say no more about them.

Let us assume that what we call an existent [*étant*] – in Heidegger's sense of the term – is a multiplicity, and that we are concerned with the appearance of that existent, which means that we can say of this existent that it reveals itself in a determinate world. Let us assume that we attempt to think that existent, but not simply in terms of its being, or in other words in terms of the pure multiplicity that constitutes its generic or indeterminate being, but attempt to think it in so far as it is there – this is the phenomenological gesture *par excellence* – and therefore in so far as it happens in this world or appears on the horizon of that world. Let us agree, like so many others before us, to call this appearance of this being in a world its *existence*.

The technical elaboration of a new (and completely rational) distinction between being and existence can take various forms, and going into detail is out of the question here. I will simply say that the relationship between being and being-there, or the relationship between multiplicity and inscription in the world, is a transcendental relationship. It consists in the fact that any multiplicity is assigned a degree of existence in the world, a degree of appearance. The fact of existing, *qua* appearing in a determinate world, is inevitably associated with a certain degree of appearance in that world, with an intensity of appearance, which we can also call intensity of existence.

There is a very complicated but very important point here, and Derrida has written a great deal about it and has taught us a lot about it: a multiplicity can appear in several different worlds. Its being-one can have a multiple existence. We accept the principle of the ubiquity of being, to the extent that it exists. A multiplicity can therefore appear or, which is the same thing, exist, in several worlds, but as a general rule it exists in those worlds with different degrees of intensity. It appears intensely in one world, more feebly in another, extremely feebly in a third, and with extraordinary intensity in a fourth. In existential terms, we are perfectly familiar with this circulation through several worlds in which we are inscribed with differentiated intensities. What we call 'life' or 'our life' is often a transition from a world in which we appear with a lower degree of existence to a world in which our degree of existence is much more intense. That is what a moment of life, a lived experience, is.

The basic point that leads us to Derrida is, then, the following: Given a multiplicity that appears in a world, and given the elements of that multiplicity, which appear along with it – this means that the totality of what constitutes it appears in that world – there is always one component in that multiplicity whose appearance is measured by the lowest degree.

This point is of extreme importance. Let me repeat it. A multiplicity appears in a world, and the transcendental relationship confers upon that multiplicity's elements degrees of appearance, degrees of existence. And it so happens that at least one of those elements – in reality, there is only one – appears with the lowest degree of appearance, or in other words has a minimal existence.

You can easily understand that having a minimal existence in the transcendental of a world is tantamount to having no existence at all there. From the world's point of view, existing as little as possible is the same as not existing at all. If you are in the world, existing as little as possible means not existing at all. That is why we describe that element as 'non-existent'.

Given a multiplicity that appears in a world, there will therefore always be an element in that multiplicity that is a non-existent in that world. A non-existent cannot be characterized in ontological terms, but only in existential terms: it is a minimal degree of existence in any determinate world.

I give you a massive and very well-known example, an example on which Derrida did a lot of work. In Marx's analysis of bourgeois or capitalist societies, the proletariat is truly the non-existent characteristic of political multiplicities. It is 'that which does not exist'. That does not mean that it has no being by any means. Marx does not think for a moment that the proletariat has no being, as he will, on the contrary, write volume after volume to explain what it is. The social and economic being of the proletariat is not in doubt. What is in doubt, always has been, and is now so more than ever, is its political *existence*. The proletariat is that which has been completely removed from political representation. The multiplicity that it is can be analysed but, if we take the rules of appearance in the political world, it does not appear there. It is there, but with a minimal degree of appearance, or in other words a degree zero of appearance. That is obviously what the *Internationale* sings: 'We are nothing, let us be all.' What does 'we are nothing' mean? Those who proclaim 'we are nothing' are not asserting their nothingness. They are simply stating that they are nothing in the world as it is, when it comes to appearing politically. From the point of view of their political appearance, they are nothing. And becoming 'all' presupposes a change of world, or in other words a change of transcendental. The transcendental must change if the ascription of an existence, and therefore a non-existence or the point of a multiplicity's non-appearance in a world, is to change in its turn.

Let us put an abrupt end to these preliminaries. One of the general laws of appearance or of being-there-in-a-world is that there is always such a point of non-existence.

I can now identify what is at stake in Derrida's thought, what is at stake in strategic terms, what is at stake in the sense that Bergson says that philosophers have only one idea. In my view, what is at stake in Derrida's work, in his never-ending work, in his writing, ramified as it is into so many varied works, into infinitely varied approaches, is the *inscription of the non-existent*. And the recognition, in the work of inscribing the non-existent, that its inscription is, strictly speaking, impossible. What is at stake in Derrida's writing – and here 'writing' designates a thought-act – is *the inscription of the impossibility of the non-existence as the form of its inscription*.

What does 'deconstruction' mean? Towards the end of his life, Derrida liked very much to say that, if there was one thing that had to be deconstructed as a matter of urgency, it was deconstruction, the word deconstruction. Deconstruction had become something in the academic repertory. To give it a meaning was, in a certain sense, to misappropriate it. I still think that, for him, the word 'deconstruction' had not been academicized at all. It was an indication of a speculative desire, a desire for thought. A basic desire for thought. That was 'his' deconstruction. And that desire, like any desire, began with an encounter, an acknowledgement. Like all the structuralists of the 1960s, like Foucault for example, Derrida accepted that the experience of the world is always an experience of discursive imposition. To be in the world is to be marked by discourses, marked even in our flesh, body, sex and so on. Derrida's thesis, Derrida's conclusion, the source of Derrida's desire is that, whatever form that discursive imposition may take, there is a point that escapes that imposition, and that we can call a vanishing point [*point de fuite*]. I think that, here, the expression has to be taken in the most literal of senses. A vanishing point is a point which, of course, flees the rule of the *dispositif* of imposition.

On that basis, the interminable work of thought, or of writing, is to locate that point. Locating it does not meaning grasping it. Because grasping it would destroy it. And so long as it is vanishing, you cannot grasp it. We can call the following problem 'Derrida's problem': what is grasping a fleeing [*fuite*]? Not grasping that which flees, not at all. But grasping fleeing *qua* vanishing point. The difficulty, which means that you always have to start again, is that, if you grasp fleeing, you suppress it at the same time. The vanishing point cannot be grasped *qua* vanishing point. It can only be located.

There is in Derrida something like the suggestion of a gesture of monstration. A gesture of writing, when writing is the finger, soaked in white ink that delicately shows the vanishing point, and at the same time lets it flee. You cannot show it 'as' a vanishing point, cannot show it dead. That is obviously what Derrida fears above all else. Showing the dead vanishing point. Showing the vanishing point in its flight. So you have a writing that will attempt to be that monstration. I call that a localization. Because to show is to locate. And to say: 'Shush . . . perhaps it's there . . . careful! Perhaps it's there . . . don't make it stop . . . let it flee . . .'

Derrida is the opposite of a hunter. A hunter hopes that the animal will stop, so that he can shoot. Or so that he can mow down the animal's flight. Derrida, however, hopes that the flight will not cease fleeing, that we can show the 'thing' (the vanishing point) in all the obviousness of its never-ending flight. And, therefore, in its incessant disappearing. What is at stake, in scriptural terms, in Derrida's desire is that all appearance is supported by (dis)appearance, and that the only aspect of it that we can locate in the forest of meaning is its endless flight.

Even locating the vanishing point – to say nothing of its seizure, which would mean its death – is in reality impossible. Because the vanishing point is that which, when it is in place, is outside-place [*hors-lieu*]. It is the outside-place in place. As it exists in its act only to the extent that it is outside-place when it is in place, we therefore cannot succeed in locating it accurately either. You want to show its fleeing, and in order to do so you must plunge deep into the forest that localizes its fleeing. And as you walk on, you learn that you can at most not show the flight, but show, from quite a distance, the sight of its fleeing: a thicket, a clearing. And that in itself is very risky.

What might, finally, be possible is to restrict the room for flight, to scour the forest more steadily, or a little less obscurely. Whilst you cannot grasp flight, localization consists simply in ensuring that the discursive imposition, the constraints of being, are not such that the space of its fleeing covers everything. Because, if that were the case, you would not be able to locate anything that is non-existent. You simply have the space of generality. But you still have to restrict the

space of your walking in order to get as close as possible
to where it flees. You must, in other words, be as close
as possible to that which excepts itself from any place,
to that which stands *hors-lieu*. Deconstruction actually
consists in so restricting discursive operations as to
allow the space of flight to be located, as in cartography,
by saying: the treasure is there . . . or, the spring is
there . . . What is disappearing is there . . . but, softly,
softly . . . otherwise the treasure will be stolen . . . the
spring will dry up . . . I have a plan, but it's vague,
vague enough to avoid stepping on the treasure . . . put
one foot on the treasure, and it is worthless . . . even
chance is dangerous . . . softly . . .

You take, for example, the great metaphysical
oppositions. We will have to diagonalize them.
Because restricting discursive space means leaving
no massivity, no linear massivity. Binary oppositions
cannot possibly locate the *hors-lieu* in any *lieu*.
So, we will have to deconstruct them. We will have
to cut across them. That is what deconstruction is.
Deconstruction is, basically, the set of operations that
can bring about a certain restriction of the space of
flight, or of the space of the vanishing point. Once
again, this is an operation that resembles an inverted

hunt. A hunt in which what we have to catch is the healthy animal that disappears, grasp the animal's bound out of any place. That is why we have to get as close to it as possible. But perhaps much closer than we need to be in order to shoot. So you have to patiently locate it. That presupposes an elementary cartography of the great distinctions between town and countryside, mountains and valleys, being and existent, and the grid-pattern must therefore gradually be reduced in scale.

Hence a whole series of discussions. The discussion with Heidegger, for example, about the real import of the difference between being and existent. When Derrida outlines the concept of 'différance' he wants to suggest a single term that can activate the being/existent distinction in its vanishing point. Derrida *puts to flight* what remains of a metaphysical opposition in the being/existent difference in such a way that we can grasp difference as such, *in its act*. And différance in action is obviously that which stands at the vanishing point of any opposition between being and existent, that which cannot in any sense be reduced to the figure of that opposition. And then we have to examine the democracy/totalitarianism opposition in the same way. Or the real impact of the Jew/Arab opposition on the Palestinian conflict. When he takes a stance on the Jew/Arab opposition in the Palestinian conflict, he once again deconstructs its duality.

The method always consists in finding what identifies a place as the territory of a vanishing point with respect to the opposition that prematurely certifies the place as a division, as a partition, as a classification.

Derrida un-closes closed matters.

In all the questions in which he intervened, Derrida was what I call a brave man of peace. He was brave because it takes a lot of courage not to enter into the division as it is constituted. And he was a man of peace because identifying what excepts itself from that opposition is, as a general rule, the road to peace. For any true peace is based upon an agreement not about that which exists, but about that which non-exists.

This diagonal obstinacy, this rejection of abrupt metaphysically derived divisions, is obviously not suited to stormy times when everything comes under the law of decisiveness, here and now. That is what kept Derrida apart from the truth of the red years between 1968 and 1976. Because the truth of those years spoke its name with the words: 'One divides into two.' What we desired, in poetic terms, was the metaphysics of radical conflict, and not the patient deconstruction of oppositions. And Derrida could not agree about that. He had to go away. He went into exile, so to speak.

The thing is, there was a great speculative gentleness about him, and it was homogeneous with his literal patience, even though he was no stranger to the violence of all real patience. There was such a thing as a Derridean touch. His great book on/ with Jean-Luc Nancy was entitled *Le Toucher* [*On Touching*]. A very beautiful book from 2000. It is his 'Treatise on the Soul', his treatise on the senses, his most delicately Aristotelian book. In it, Derrida tries to give a new description of the relationship between the physical world and thought. Once again, you have to find what stands at the vanishing point of the opposition between the physical world and thought. There is something of the kind in the sense of touch. A something so delicately physical that it becomes indistinguishable from thought.

Derrida became increasingly fond of the dialogue form for the same reason. Dialogues with Hélène Cixous, Elisabeth Roudinesco, Habermas or others. And especially a dialogue with what might be called the feminine position. In a dialogue with a heteronomous position, you will, perhaps, touch that which flees the Law, that which supplely bounds out of the *nomos*. You will caress it in passing. That passing touch corresponds very profoundly to Derrida's philosophical desire.

What do we want to do with it when we desire something? This non-existent, this desire, this desire for the non-existent, must, ultimately and of necessity, be couched [*il faut le coucher*]. Couched on a blank sheet of paper, for example. Even though we know that it is already back on its feet. It is already elsewhere. It is already gone. Such was Derrida's desire: locate, touch, clasp, even for less than an instant, the non-existent of a place, the vanishing of the vanishing point. Inscribe its ex-scription.

That went against philosophical custom, for which the basis of non-existence is nothingness. Now, you cannot, absolutely cannot, say of the inexistent that it is nothingness. That is the whole problem. That is where the metaphysical error lies, the only metaphysical error that is irremediable. The metaphysical error *par excellence* is to have identified the non-existent with nothingness. Because the point is that the non-existent *is*. That is why proletarians, who non-exist, can argue, on the basis of their being, that 'We are nothing, let us be all.' That is the very definition of Revolution: a non-existent uses its being-multiple in order to declare that it will exist in the absolute sense. And for that to happen, we have to change the world of course, change the world's transcendental.

The non-existent is *nothing*. But being nothing is by no means the same as not-being. To be nothing is to non-exist in a way specific to a determinate world or place. The alternating slippages characteristic of Derrida's prose thus become clear. The slippage between 'if you say that the non-existent *is*, you naturally fail to see this: that it does not exist', and 'if you simply say that it does not exist, you fail to see this: that it *is*'. And therefore, no stable opposition can really succeed in describing the precise status of the non-existent in terms of a binary opposition. Because you always slip from being to non-existence, and then from non-existence to being. So much so that, with Derrida, you have a logic that is no longer authorized by the basic distinction between assertion and negation.

I think this is the crux of the matter. Deconstruction is taken to its limit when the logical space in which you are operating is no longer that of the opposition between assertion and negation at all. I would that this is what touching is. When you touch something, you are that thing, and you are not that thing. That is the whole tragedy of the loving caress. Relating to a text, or a political situation, in the way that the loving caress logically relates to a body: that is deconstruction's ideal. Touching's ideal. In touching, that which touches is separate from that which is touched only by a non-existence, a non-ascribable vanishing point. For the distinction between the two '*actants*' involved in touching – the active and the passive – is merely the act of touching, which is, of course, also what conjoins them. That is the major slippage, the slippage that has as its sign, its hitching post, the non-existent.

Derrida installed this slippage in language. This will be my last remark. He tried to say that any real world is a slippage. A word is not a reference, is not a signifier; it is a slippage, a slippage between being and existence. A word rings true when it slips or slides in time with the non-existent. 'Slide mortals, do not insist',[1] I think that is what Derrida was saying when

1   *Glissez mortels, n'insistez pas*. Translator's note: The allusion is to a quatrain by the librettist Pierre-Charles Roy (1683–1764): '*Glissez mortels, n'appuyez pas*' ('Slide, mortals, do not press down'). It is about ice-skating.

he wrote his own words. That is why he has been much criticized. Sometimes even I was irritated by his extraordinary verbal acrobatics, his derivations, the endless sliding of his prose. But we can, must, do justice to all that, as the monstration of the slippage supports the desire for the non-existent. You must demonstrate the vanishing point by making language free. You must have a language of flight. You can only organize a monstration of the non-existent if you use a language that can stand non-existing. A language of flight. And in that case, as Genet used to say, 'My victory is verbal.'

My ultimate tribute will also be verbal.

In tribute to Derrida, I will henceforth write 'inexistence' with an *'a'*. Inexist*a*nce. In the same way that he said différ*a*nce. And basically getting very close to what he meant when, a long time ago, he invented the word 'différance'. The word différance is basically the operation whereby Derrida tries to couch non-existence. To couch in the way you couch something in writing. He tried to couch the non-existent in différance as an act of writing, as a slippage. Learning from him, I too will try to couch non-existence by inflicting upon it the slippage from 'e' to 'a', which signifies, in its worldly way of non-existing, that its being is no less reducible for that. We are nothing, let us be all. That is the imperative of non-existance. There is no way out of that. I thank Jacques Derrida for having been the vigilant keeper of that imperative.

Jean Borreil (1938–1992)*

There is something muted and grating, something stubborn, about Jean Borreil's writing, just as there was in the power of his voice, and the word 'style' does not really capture it.[1]

And besides, Borreil was suspicious of style. What his thought dislikes above all else is stability, arrogance and conventional decency. Now propriety easily becomes a matter of style. He writes: 'We tolerate the moral order, even racism, provided that it can tart itself up in a style that inscribes it in a semblance of decorum.' For Borreil, style is often a way of dressing up abjection. But perhaps the whole point of his own

* Editorial note: Jean Borreil was a writer, playwright and professor in the Department of Philosophy of the Université de Paris 8. His works include *La Raison nomade* (1993) and, co-edited with Jacques Rancière, *Les Sauvages dans la cité: Auto-émancipation du peuple et instruction des prolétaires au XIXe siècle* (1985).

1 The references are to *La Raison nomade*, Paris: Payot-Rivages, 1993.

style is to outwit arrogance. He discovered a singular gentleness in the way thought settles down, in its journey, or in its smiling but definitive pressure.

Starting, probably, with the extraordinary role he gives to interrogation. I say interrogations, not questions. There is no investigative hermeneutics in Borreil, but there are countless question marks, and they are material. These punctuation marks ask you, together with the author in question, to sum up the questions, but also to take your bearings [*faire le point*], to describe the point of the journey and the position [*point*] of the nomad in the world, as he describes it. It is that of the exile on the spot, the motif of the equality of singularities.

His writing abounds in interrogations, but not because his thought has taken a break from its great interrogation of meaning and destiny. On the contrary, it abounds in interrogations because it invites us to move immediately in the direction of an internal and unpredictable halt. The interrogation is always faithfully followed by an answer. It is there to signal that the answer is what we have to move towards, that it is not an already-there that is unveiled or revealed. The answer is the possibility of a shared moment. When Borreil asks, 'What is the intolerable?' he immediately replies: 'That which provokes a rejection and an insurrection'. When he asks, speaking of Hyperion, 'Why does knowledge fail?' he replies: 'Because reflection cannot dissolve dissonances'. Even the well-known founding anecdote is initiated by an interrogation. In order to remind us of the scandalous invention of Diogenes the Cynic, he uses narrative and its interpretation. He asks: 'What is this philosophical act *par excellence*?' And he replies: 'Diogenes masturbating in the marketplace'. And then he asks: 'What lesson does this teach us?' And immediately replies, as though he himself were a schoolboy who has been asked by an intimate but strict master to think, to think for himself: 'The lesson, for the Greeks of the time, is this novel paradox: the marketplace is my bedroom, the public space is a private space.' According to this interrogation, thought is forced to weigh anchor and to set sail on an uncertain sea; thought is for itself that quasi-other that everyone is, in Borreil's view, for everyone else. The nomadic image is inscribed from the outset in that singular style, which never asserts anything except under the rule of an interrogation, and interposes between the interrogation and the response the interval between the morning departure and the evening halt.

His style of thought therefore relates to the sea and to ports. For the enemy of thought is constantly identified by Borreil as the rightful owner. The owner of the Polis, of goods, the owner of politics and, ultimately, the would-be owner of thought itself. The enemy of thought has settled on its lands, has appropriated in the proper sense, is a proper-ty owner [*propre-iétaire*]. The thought that is associated with the sea and with ports dispossesses the proper-ty owner. And Borriel then asks:

> Are not ports a space for merchants and 'capitalists' who always put their personal salvation before the salvation of the *polis?* Are they not a space of prostitution and night, and the very opposite of the sun that floods the agonistic debates of the agora with its light? In short, are not ports the image of, even an earthly substitute for, the Cosmopolis?

The point is that, according to Borreil, thought follows a wandering and difficult line, and has no fixed points to steer by. It plots its position [*fait le point*] without any ideal sun. It is primarily a thought without any vertical, a thought that moves in the purely horizontal plane of equality.

The modern city is the emblem of that plane of immanence. Borreil says: 'A city, a pure surface'. Or in other words, the explicit opposite of 'Heideggerian and poetic land': 'the horizontality of a city, trampled in all directions without making sense'. Joyce's Dublin, the 'nowhere' attested to by the modern writer he loved and read more than any other.

I will say that thought must avoid two things: the loop [*boucle*] and the overhang [*surplomb*]. Only the avoidance of the two can entrust thought to the horizontality of the site of quasi-others, to the equality of fellows.

Avoiding loops takes many forms in Borreil. We will say first that thought must proceed on a local basis, and that it presupposes no general movement that might take it back to a supposedly originary motif. What we do have are in fact local disasters, things that happen and to which we stubbornly bear witness. Thought adapts itself to this as best it can. It asks: 'How can we adapt speech [*une parole*] to a series of disasters?' Adapting it establishes a style that always

proceeds from one point to another, without it ever
being a matter of making general inferences. In that
respect, nothing could be more striking that the truly
stylistic use he makes of references, of proper names.
We have here a maximal improbability, a surprise, a
sort of theft of names. And, besides, he says: we must
have 'a relationship with the history of philosophy, a
relationship that is not one of erudition, but one of
distortion and capture, if not theft'.

From the history of philosophy, but not only from
that. Take *L'Impossible retour à Ithaque*. We begin
with Homer and the Odyssey, and the critique in
the *Traité du sublime*. For, let it be said in passing,
Borreil knows a lot of things, knows everything. Then
the motifs of the oriental, and of sobriety, suddenly
make us change course and steer for Hölderlin, for
Kleist.

In the background, we can glimpse Goethe and
Schiller. The question of the voyage, which is that of
the movement of thought, becomes more acute: 'the
voyage is a disaster'. The destruction of the proper
has been announced: 'The same question of going
home; but there is no longer any home to go to.' So
we ask what makes the return of Ulysses possible,

and it is the crucial episode of the Sirens, which takes us to a port that nothing could have predicted: Michel Foucault. This is about traversing suffering and death. And it is with a wrench that we read the central phrase, another interrogation and its answer: 'What remains to be done when we have traversed death? Go home.' This connection between traversing death and the return evokes Hegel, who leads us via caesurae and localizations, via Tübingen to Hyperion, to Hölderlin, to the elegies to the setting sun. And the Mediterranean is finally abolished in favour of Joyce's urban horizontality.

There is nothing anarchic or botched about this. A point to point navigation that hugs the shore, that holds on to what it has won, and nothing more. Borreil's style of thought takes as its maxim Rimbaud's maxim: 'Hold on to what you have not won.' That alone guarantees that we will not be seduced by the sirens of the loop, of the Totality.

He says so of Joyce, but Joyce is a buoy for his own navigation: 'Neither reflexive language nor the Odyssean march of consciousness, but Molly Bloom's monologue.' The monologue is the answer to the loop. To be understood in the sense of that which on its own accord goes towards the affirmative Alteration of the self. The monologue of the loss of the proper, of the absence of an end, of the ratification of the quasi-other.

Its maxim is that there is no return, that there is only loss, and that loss is our modern freedom, the freedom that is, if we can put it this way, unbuckled or un-looped [*débouclée*]. We will put it this way: 'We never return to Ithaca. We do not get lost so as to find ourselves once more but, and this is the whole point, so as to get lost.' Rimbaud again, the Rimbaud who said: 'We do not leave.' Borreil would say, rather: 'Oh yes we do!' The problem is that we do not come back [*revenir*], that we do not get over it [*en revenir*]. But the other trap to be avoided is that of the overhang. The style of thought that means so much to Borreil is a repudiation of the universal. For the universal is nothing more than disguised arrogance on the part of the proper, of what is proper to the West. That is what defines a twofold stylistic wager: a wager on the singularity of prose, and a wager on its similitude and vocation for sharing. But in order to reach that crucial point, we have an avalanche of questions:

What are we to do with these dissimilar fellows?
What are we do to with a distress that is covered
up by words? How are we to discover what is
intolerable about a continual disaster, a continual
destruction? What word are we to keep because it
is not encircled, as they say of the West in Africa,
if not 'tiring'?

And, just the once won't hurt, the answer takes the
form of an imperative: 'We must wager against the
universalism that expresses an arrogance, and yet still
maintain the primacy of equality amongst fellows.'
This imperative that conjoins two wagers that are
in themselves dangerous, but whose conjunction
is still more dangerous, governs his whole style,
the interrogation, local navigation, the ports, the
unexpected way the sky is filled with starry names, the
obstinacy, the monologue. . .

   Is this in fact thought, or an endless exposition?
Borreil states: 'Thinking the plural may be an
impossibility.' Now the thought of the plural is indeed
the content of the egalitarian imperative, and of the
repudiation of universalism. Let us say that his style
is the shared exposition of the plural, which is itself

secretly pluralized by an impossible thought. The text, which is governed by this tension, must retain something of the aleatory. It must be the trace of a chance occurrence, of an encounter, of what has been registered whilst trampling horizontality.

I salute – and I quote – 'the attention to the aleatory nature of a gaze that does not decide a priori what is worth looking at and what is not'.

The style of his thought is to make this non-decision apparent. A non-decision that is not indecision, but a bifurcated trajectory, the local advent of prose's drift. So that in the end we are not where we imagine we are going. We have been damaged and, like planes in the mist, diverted to a foreign land. Which also means we are at home, as this diversion reveals to us the impropriety of the proper, the alterity of the native, the breaking of all loops and the impossibility of all overhangs.

I recall the time when I had sharp political disagreements with Jean Borreil. Leaving aside the terminology of the day, I should imagine that he was really criticizing me for deciding too far in advance what was worth looking at. The point is that his style of thought was not, all in all, that of a politics in the usual sense. Nor that of a philosopher. He was a philosopher, but not a philosopher of philosophy. He looked more like a witness. In his thought, the balance between singularity and similitude is too fine to be found. Rather than taking an interest in the pointless odysseys of the concept, he was preoccupied with finding the local point, the cosmopolitan port from where we can hear – hear properly – the discourse of the other. Speaking of François Châtelet, he used to say: 'Respect and disrespect: that is the non-romantic way to listen to the reasons of the other.'

And that, ultimately, is what it is about: a non-romantic style of thought, a dismissal of all the heroes of the concept, an assured patience, a fraternal ploughing. And I will let him say, in conclusion, of Claude Simon, but also of himself, what he wanted the writing of thought to do:

Take centre-stage in order to disrupt it and perhaps, in the way that the October wind of a nameless country strips the vines of their leaves, to strip the bride bare and exhibit her in a picture.

Philippe Lacoue-Labarthe (1940–2007)

With him, all things took on a singular profundity.[1] Not the profundity of pathos, nor that of the obscure. A loyal profundity, I would like to say, that was like my experience of his friendship: reserved, sustained by few facts, almost distant, and yet absolutely steady. Yes, there was a steadiness about Philippe Lacoue-Labarthe, and it was strangely homogeneous with the strange lack of consolation one senses in a man who was always disconsolate because the world has not yet succeeded in being what it is. Inconsolable and steady, and profound because it is absolutely steady; such was his thought, such as I read it, such as I understand it.

1 References in this chapter are to the following works by Lacoue-Labarthe: *L'Imitation des modernes*, Paris: Galilée, 1986; *La Poésie comme expérience*, Paris: Christian Bourgois, 1997; *Musica ficta (Figures de Wagner)*, Paris: Christian Bourgois, 1991; *La Fiction du politique*, Paris: Christian Bourgois, 1988.

He had of course retained, not to say transformed, Heidegger's maxim to the effect that the essence of thought is the question. He clung to that maxim, because it seems to me that two questions organize what he refused to call philosophical 'theses', though they are still theses in the movement of their incessant experimentation. The question of Auschwitz, yes, reworked, reworked, beyond Adorno, in such a way that we can use it as a starting point for an accurate assessment of the relationship between that monstrosity and the speculative genealogy of the West, Heidegger included. And then, included and distinct, the question of the poem and of its own mode of possible innocence, as indicated by the non-poetic interiority of the poem, or its idle essence, which we can also call its becoming-prose. His questions lie, in a word, between the two poles of our historial site. The first: the complicity of a lethal politics and the configuring will of great art, a complicity organized by the work of art's mimetic motif. The second: the poetic possibility of withdrawal, as indicated by an art that escapes any will to contour it and all monumentality. An art that can exist after all great art. The mediation between the two was the complication of theatre, perdition and salvation.

Within this marked space, in which we all reside, he
shored up the work of his two questions with struggles
that were as explicit as they were singular. Therein
lay his inimitable style: harsh and rounded, but also
with a gentleness to it, like an embrace, a constraint.
To that extent, he went beyond Heidegger's vision of
questionability.

In order to discover completely the mimetic
and mythological nature of what gives speculative
genealogy its monstrosity, the critique of great art
must be taken to its logical conclusion. Which means
that we must go far beyond what Nietzsche intuited,
namely the aphrodisiac harmfulness of Wagner.
We have to show that not only Wagnerism, but also
most attempts to rival Wagner, or to outdo him, are
inscribed with an artistic fictioning [*fictionnement*]
that is consonant with the fiction of the political.
And therefore, in genealogical terms, contemporary
with the disaster. *Musica ficta (Figures de Wagner)*
and *La Fiction du politique*: two essential books by
Philippe. Wagner is, so to speak, the name of the
site where the first question can be tried out. The
question of fiction, which is the question of fascism
as thought at work.

And then, at the other pole, the poem has to be wrested away from Heidegger's great, memorable interpretation, which, even at the height of its distress, traps it into the will to configure, still and always. And this time, it is Hölderlin and Paul Celan who are affirmatively decisive.

Let us praise in passing the extreme precision of our dead friend. Broad as the questions may be, he always assigns them to perfectly circumscribed places: a task, a phrase, a surprising connection between authors who are far apart, an episode . . . And he persuades us, by sober means and with steady, thoughtful gestures, that this is indeed the place of time and space, the fragment of the prose of the world in which we can concentrate the question. And one of these extremely difficult tasks, and a major philosophical desire on his part, is to wrest Hölderlin away from Heidegger. To wrest Heidegger away from that powerful hermeneutics, which is some respects paradoxically definitive, and which was almost that poet's first discovery. Discovering Hölderlin for a second time; that is one possible name for the passion of Philippe Lacoue-Labarthe. And elsewhere, an episode inscribed in a text: understanding and saying what is said and crypted in Paul Celan's poem *Todtnauberg* gives, as we know, an account of the encounter between Heidegger and Celan. Philippe says of this poem that it is scarcely a poem, that it is a becoming-prose, in which the radical disjunction between the experience of poetry and the way the will to configure enframes[2] poetry, transcends all form. To understand that transit is to understand the poetic exception with respect to that which supports monstrosity. And all that provides the substance of two other crucial books by Philippe: first, *L'Imitation des modernes*, with 'La Césure du spéculatif', one of the most astonishing texts of recent decades, and that other but no less radical text, *Hölderlin et les Grecs*, which, yes, really is the compulsory Bible for anyone investigating the linked destinies of philosophy, drama and the poem. And then *La Poésie comme expérience* [*Poetry as Experience*], a solitary and tormented book that finally takes stock of Celan.

I would like to say here, and to explain, what I wrote to Jean-Luc Nancy as soon as the news of

2   Translator's note: the French term used is *arraisonner*, which refers to the boarding of a ship to inspect its cargo for customs purposes. It is used to translate Heidegger's *das Gestell*, normally translated into English as 'enframing'.

Philippe's death reached me in California. That I felt myself to be in mourning in two senses. In mourning for him, and for all that he gave us, loyally, profoundly. And in mourning for what he had not yet been able to give us. Because, cruelly, he was in some way prevented from doing so whenever his essential non-inconsolability came into conflict with the clarification of these questions. A virtual mourning, in a word, in addition to my immediate mourning, like some supernumerary pain.

The point is that Philippe was constantly working on the future of these questions. It is not that he was a man for deferral or interminable promises. Not at all. But he did fling clear, almost peremptory phrases, and assertory, trenchant formulae, into the future as though he were throwing clear pebbles into dark water. Those statements, those formulae, did not always have their full trappings, their subtle legitimation or their experimental supports. But they would have had them sooner or later in the discontinuous and rigorous deployment of his experience of thought and writing. I also mourn having to live with those acute expectations, having been struck by these sentences, having been awoken, turned over and abandoned by the effect of death, which closes them as they are projected towards something that we may never understand. We can cite here some of Philippe Lacoue-Labarthe's 'sayings', though their truth is henceforth restricted to an obviousness that goes beyond its immediate context.

In *L'Imitation des modernes*: 'The tragic begins with the ruin of the imitable.' 'Beginning the Greeks again means that we are no longer Greek at all.' 'Heidegger's political sin is the abandonment of the tragic.' And this, which we can at least read from inside our pain: 'God is dead. Translate: God is me.'

In *La Poésie comme expérience*: 'What a poem recounts is that from which it wrests itself insofar as it is a poem.' 'Poetry is the interruption of art.' 'Any poem is always too beautiful, even one by Celan.' And this, which also has a singular ring to it today: 'Art after the end of art shows the pain of showing. That might be joy itself.'

In *Musica ficta (Figures de Wagner)*: 'No aesthetics or artistic practice can declare itself innocent of a politics.' 'Wagner's music is a figural music.' '[It is incumbent on us to go to] that place where we stubbornly tried to articulate and bind together (or bind together again) art and politics. We still have to destroy the figure as the concept of that binding.' And finally this, which, despite everything of which Philippe accuses Wagner, I will identity with his adversary, and identify us with that perverse magician's successors: 'Wagner's work bequeaths his posterity an impossible task: going on with what has been completed.'

If I had to recall only one of these many sayings that were thrown into the future of thought, and, first and foremost, into that of his own thought, it would, perhaps, be one that I have cited many times and which, in the pure present of our history, sounds like a warning that is as obvious and violent as it is difficult to tolerate: 'Nazism is a humanism.'

Whether or not we agree, this has to do with the Wagnerian wager: 'go on with what has been completed'. We have to argue, against him, that this great art is not supported by a mythology, that its proto-fascism is no more certain than the claim that Hölderlin was trapped by Heidegger's configuring will, that Wagner's real destination is still in abeyance, still ahead of us, after a long sequence of diversions. That, basically, Lacoue-Labarthe is, in negative terms, what Heidegger is to Hölderlin in positive terms: the damaged support for a historial construct. And so, following the trail of white pebbles he threw ahead of himself, he would have replied, and we would have gone on, squabbling in a friendship which was also lucid, distant, profound. But he is dead. Today, suffice it to say that we mourn for what he has given us, that we mourn for that quarrel and all the others that he stirred up, in friendship and with firmness, which have not taken place, and in the course of which he would have told us, as a bonus, the secret of donation itself.

Gilles Châtelet (1945–1999)*

Is it possible to forget his approach, to leave it behind the text? Is it possible not to relate this avid, complex prose to his way, at once reserved and predatory, of sidling into the speculative arena? I think not. I want to say it to end this colloquium: Gilles Châtelet's prose is not that of just any essayist. And still less is it that of an epistemologist. An epistemologist is someone who, by turning science into the history of the sciences, and the history of the sciences into an object that is divorced from philosophy, kills, quite simply, both the vitality of the sciences and their ability to grasp philosophy. Gilles

---

* Editorial note: Gilles Châtelet taught philosophy at the Université de Paris 8. His works include *Figuring Space: Philosophy, Mathematics and Physics* [*Les enjeux du mobile: mathématique, physique, philosophie*, 1993], Dordecht, Boston and London: Kluwer Academic Publishers, 2000 and *Vivre et penser comme des porcs: de l'incitation à l'envie et à l'ennui dans les démocraties-marchés* (1999).

Châtelet would have said 'Open fire on epistemology!' in many different ways. That was one of many ways of saying 'Long live philosophy!' He would have said that because he was at once a mathematician, a physicist, a historian and a philosopher. But he would also have said it because he was tragically homosexual and depressively ill. He would have said it with the instinct he sensed within himself, the instinct of what he himself called 'a clear-sighted queer' and of a sick man for whom the life of the concept was also thought's race against death. And he would have said 'Open fire on epistemology!' by weaving the tenuous and reversible link between science and philosophy that he called the dialectic. And perhaps 'Open fire on epistemology!' meant, first of all, that thought, or scientific thought, is caught in a body's gestural capacity. And that explaining that gestural capacity requires a speculative monumentality whose form was established once and for all by Hegel or Schelling. We have to go from the most intimate gesture, the most delicate algebraic writing, to the universal mobility of that which exists. That is why we cannot – it would be a detestable abuse – divorce Gilles Châtelet's text from the singular capacity of his body, or from the sarcastic insolence of his voice. Between the body and the text . . . style, a prose that is both that of a man firing a revolver and that of a lace maker.

And so we will put forward the hypothesis, which is internal to his way of being and thinking, that what wore out Gilles Châtelet was an excessive body, a concern for the self that was too introverted, insufficiently dialectical, too remote from the power to write. The tragedies, which were terrible, and the exhaustion, which was barren, divorced his body from its capacity for writing. So the divorce has to be taken to extremes. Go away. I say that that calm disjunction, which was very meditated, was romantically faithful in this sense: the body must pass away because it no longer exists within a live tension with thought. Yes, the body passes away because it is dialectically unavailable.

And so we ask ourselves, as a starting point and in tribute to a life and a death, what the dialectic meant to him. It is quite clear from *Figuring Space* that the dialectic is not the synthetic neutralization of two pre-existing but contradictory terms, but the discovery of the articulation that deploys the dimension along which they suddenly emerge as 'sides'. The word 'articulation' is one of Châtelet's key-signifiers. It designates the active unity of an operation as a preliminary to any determination of a duality; the dialectic is indeed 'one divides into two' and not 'two is extenuated into one'. But it has to be understood that the One is no more than one dimension that is unfolded by the latent play of an articulation that is still there before One is divorced from Two. The dialectic is never a dualized sequence of concepts. The dialectic is the polarization of a space that is articulated. That is why Gilles Châtelet could, and had to, constantly go back to that philosophy of nature of German romanticism, with its obsession with magnetic poles, attraction and repulsion, electric polarity and elective affinities.

And if we wish to understand him, we always have to go back to that complex of dimension, articulation and the dynamic advent of duality, and to the central intuition of the moment where science works, invents and unfolds its natural fecundity. And we must do so by staying very close to examples, very close to the strokes of inspiration known as Oresme's diagrams, Grassmann's quadrilateral, Poisson's virtual sections, and Argand's laterals. This scholarly proximity does not construct any history of the sciences; it simply tries to think the epic of scientific thought. There is in Gilles Châtelet a constant desire not to stand outside a science as it exists. His goal is, yes, to rediscover and write the subjectivity of knowledge, the gestures it makes not when it is being taught or imposed, but when it is alone at home. And the subjectivity of science when it is 'at home' is nothing other than the dialectic, as the life of thought.

Hence, of course, Gilles Châtelet's great polemics, his imprecatory fury with all the powers of death or all indecent displays of immobility. It is no doubt a pity that the public success of the polemicist masks his central work. Provocations can sometimes resemble misunderstandings. And we should recall that this success, in which we all rejoice, did not give our close friend the inner power or the resources of joy for very long, but nor should we hide the fact that polemical vivacity is an essential component of the romantic dialectic. For, if we are to reach deep into the unfolding that creates notions, we must constantly fight false symmetries in our understanding of both time and space. Arguing that the two cannot be divorced, and mobilizing his succulent repertoire of mental insults, Gilles speaks of the 'ill-tempered clash between positive and negative' and 'trivial intuitions about the juxtaposition of parts'. Rejecting the idea of succession, he denounces 'the slavery of the transitive and spatial',[1] and, directly, the clichés of 'successivity'.[2]

It is only when we have rooted out, both within us and outside us, facile orderings, alignments and symmetries that we can gain access to the inner workings of movement. We recognize here Bergson, or Deleuze, as opposed to the *partes extra partes* of Cartesian extension. Temporal entanglement is superior to spatial spreading out, and the non-commutative is superior to symmetry, and the fold to juxtaposition. If we know that, and if we use both its polemical power and the delicacy of its investigations, then we know that any dialectical duality is folded, articulated and polarized. We know – and this is a superb formula – that 'any Two is inexorably entangled in with what envelops it'. And as our reward, we will have what Schelling called the 'tenderness' of articulation.[3] It is at this point

1   Gilles Châtelet, *Figuring Space: Philosophy, Mathematics and Physics*, p. 145.
2   Ibid., p. 78.
3   Ibid., p. 94.

that Gilles Châtelet settles into his most astonishing ability: the ability to conjure up the poetry of abstract inventions, without surrendering any of their rigour. There will always be those moments when he shows us these intimate and intense points where thought transforms indecision into a new orientation, those moments where scientific intuition is a path that divides into two.

For example, the wonderful demonstration, with reference to Grassmann, of the dialectical virtues of non-commutative algebra. Thanks to dissymmetry, a sort of geometry of the concept is haunted by literal discontinuity; whilst it never loses any of its algebraic austerity, letters themselves become geometrical, and dance, so much so that the mathematician can get a creative hold on a new kinetics. I quote: 'By linking the free-style dance of the letters to a continuum where circuits can deform one another, the geometer gains kinetic formulae.'[4] Gaining kinetic formulae and inventing a geometry of movements is of course one of the maxims of algebra. It is also, as we can sense, one of the maxims of life; the same is no doubt true of all

4   Ibid., p. 145.

the great orientations of Gilles Châtelet's thought. They are well-suited to the erudite finesse of his examples of scientific creation, but they also apply to the talents of living bodies. Because the romantic dialectic is, precisely, the body, as revealed in all its brilliance at the point where an idea becomes oriented.

I would like here to repeat what I believe to be the five major maxims of the thought of our friend by showing their links with the possible range of the life of the body. And by showing, in a word, why Gilles Châtelet was not an epistemologist; in his view, any statement about science could be converted into a maxim for life.

1. First, a motif that is, for Gilles Châtelet, much more than a speculative conviction, much more than a topos in the philosophy of the sciences. It is, I think I can say, an existential, or even political, certainty, because it is the romantic dialectic itself: thought has its roots in the body. The body conceived as dynamic spatiality. Whilst Husserl sought the vital and ante-predictive origins of geometry, Gilles Châtelet will say: 'The origins of thought are geometric.' All thought is the knotting together of a space and a gesture, if not the gestural unfolding of a space. The life maxim that corresponds to this motif can be written as: 'Unfold the

space that does justice to your body.' Gilles Châtelet's love of a night's partying obeyed that maxim. It is more ascetic than it seems because constructing pleasure's nocturnal space is at least as much a duty as a form of consent.

2. The geometric origins of thought can only be discovered if we discern in all actualization – and still more so in all literalization – the potential for articulation, which is the principle of deployment. Geometry is not the science of extrinsic extension in the Cartesian sense; it is a source for extraction and thickening, a gestural language of de-formation, a truly physical virtuality. So much so that we have to think in terms of a sort of spatial interiority, and in terms of the intrinsic virtue of variation that the thinking gesture both provokes and accompanies.

Turning to the realm of the living, it should be noted that loneliness and interiority are perhaps, alas, the subjective essence of alterity and the outside world. Gilles Châtelet knew countless people, but there was in that apparent dissemination, a hefty, and no doubt ultimately lethal, dose of loneliness and withdrawal.

3. The latent continuity is always more important than the discontinuous section: Koyré, Kuhn, Popper

and Lakatos are the apostles of discontinuity, and Châtelet sees the unity behind the apparent polemics, and their 'breaks', 'revolutions' and 'falsifiabilities' have to be contrasted with a different way of localizing thought.

That is why the 'history of ideas' dances to a different rhythm: the rhythm of 'breaks', 'paradigms' and their refutations, which is quite discontinuous, and that of problematic latencies that are always there to be reactivated and full of treasures for anyone who can awaken them.

For Châtelet, the history of thought is never already-written, already-periodized. Thought sleeps in temporal continuity. There are never anything more than singularities that can be reactivated and creative virtualities that nestle in the folds of time.

This time, the life maxim is: 'Reactivate your sleeping childhood, be the prince of your own beauty, which no one can suspect. Activate your virtuality.' In the realm of existence, we can call the drying up of the virtual 'materialism', and understand why Gilles Châtelet wanted to restore to that materialism the romantic idealism of the powers of childhood, as opposed to the *partes extra partes* of Cartesian extension.

4. Being reveals itself to thought – scientific or philosophical thought, it's all the same – in 'indifference centres'[5] that contain the ambiguity of all possible separation. That dialectical ambiguity is signalled by the de-routing [*déroute*] of spatial obviousness, which always thinks that it can find its direction and plan its walk; at the point where these indifference centres, these reversible spaces or these bascules, meet, the understanding that divides and intuition fuse into a paradoxical intensity of thought. Nothing could be more revelatory, and nothing could do more to unveil that which exists in its elegant uncertainty, than those points of maximal ambiguity where a new pact is sealed between the understanding and intuition.

This time, we will say: 'Be the dandy of ambiguities. Love only that which disrupts your order, even if it destroys you.'

5. The higher organization of thought is always the result of a combination of an axis of penetration and laterals, which are at once arrayed along the axis and orthogonal, and therefore resistant to pure laterality. Only that *dispositif* (the 'right' strength of

5   Ibid., p. 79.

the axis and the laid-out resistance of the lateral) can
grasp the multiple, or diversity. What is the multiple?
Ultimately, and for anyone who thinks, the multiple
is a product of laterality's disruption of linearity.
Speaking of Grassmann's 'capture of the extension',
Châtelet explains that the theory of extension proposes
to master the birth of what is continuously diverse.
That diversity must not be thought of as the diversity of
blocks that are extensively dispersed, and must form a
system: it must be the product of a coherent disruption.
That ambiguity therefore demands of transitivities the
most resolute, most orthogonal poetic propulsion, and
it exalts to the highest the gesture that cuts through
and exposes form. So we can see: a thought is that
which masters, thanks to a resolute gestural handling,
the most resistant literalities and the generation of
'what is continuously diverse'. Grasping being does not
convene the spreading out or the assembled presence
of the oneness of meaning; it convenes – and that is
perhaps the most important word – the irreducible
dialectic of dimensions. In that sense, thought is
never unilaterally dedicated to organized meaning,
even though Châtelet, as scrupulous as ever, always
remembers the need for letters and pure algebra.

But that is not what is ultimately at stake in thought. What is ultimately at stake lies in its ability to capture dimensionality; in order to do that, it must invent notations, and they exceed the power of the letter.

In connection with this point, romantic idealism teaches us to find, not the meaning of our existence, but its precise dimensions. To live is to invent unknown dimensions of existence and therefore, as Rimbaud used to say, 'fix those vertigos'. That, after all, is what we can learn from both the life and the death of Gilles Châtelet; we need vertigo, but we also need to give it form, or in other words fix it.

This is because vertigo is indeed what the romantic dialectic tries to find at the centre of rationality itself, to the extent that rationality is an invention and therefore a fragment of a natural power. Yes, Gilles Châtelet is always in search of the places where the understanding vacillates. It is in centres where there is no differentiation that we achieve the greatest certainty, which therefore demands the most irreversible decisiveness. That, no doubt, is the most obviously philosophical element. Constructing a dialectic of ambiguity, vertigo and vacillation. Not because it makes us hesitate but, on the contrary, so that there will be real dissymmetry, and therefore irreversible decisiveness.

And of course, it is in this correlation between ambiguity and decisiveness, indifference and reversibility, that we recognize Gilles Châtelet's filiation or speculative genealogy. We can trace it back, in the same way that we can draw a family tree that opens on to the obscurity of very ancient times.

1. Deleuze, who seeks in science the polysemic and creative richness of its function, the way a chaotic virtuality filters into a plane of reference.

2. Schelling, who tries to think intuition's intuition, the zone of communicational ambiguity that lies between art and science. Schelling, who rejected Hegel's concept because it was still too formal, too discursive, too enveloping and too self-confident.

3. There is Leibniz, the thinker of force as potentiality, the theorist of the 'labyrinth of the continuous', the man of imperceptible bifurcations and concurrent laterals. Leibniz, who argued against Descartes' *partes extra partes*.

4. Aristotle, who discovered the need to think power as power, and who placed great emphasis on the virtual, on that which is not yet quite what it is. The Aristotle

of natural dynamism, of irreducible singularity, of movement as the unfolding and first quality of physical being. Aristotle, who rejected the fixed actuality of Platonic ideality.

But all that is picked up and, as it were, set in motion and de-routed [*mise en route et en deroute*], by the style of the romantic dialectic. Its style is joyous and peremptory, but it is also detailed, labyrinthine, a sort of explosive abstraction. It is inspired by an essential desire to destroy the dispositions of Kant's transcendental aesthetic, which presupposes a brutal disjunction between space and time. Irrespective of their necessarily relativist correlation, what Châtelet, relying upon both modern algebraic geometry and the theory of dynamic systems, is asking is that we find, in the space of folds, the lack of differentiation and the knots that 'gestualize' and therefore temporalize it.

Let me say it once more: finding, or safeguarding, the ability to temporalize in contemporary mercantile space, knowing where it is still possible for the thought-body to make any gesture. Those are the important and urgent questions that lie behind Gilles Châtelet's non-epistemology.

Let us learn from one for whom one question leads from the diagrams of non-commutative algebra to the 'arborescences' of wave mechanics, just as it leads from Aristotle to Deleuze. It is an imperative question, a disturbing question, and a question that does indeed combine non-differentiation with irreversibility. It is the question of the watchman who hears in space the sound of a gesture: 'Who goes there?' He asked, asked himself, the question: 'Who goes there?' Truth to tell, he leaves us several answers, and above all several ways of answering it. In order to be true to him we will try to choose.

Françoise Proust (1947–1998)[*]

There was, after all, something severe about her attractiveness, something powerful about her delicacy, something very harsh about her delicacy.[1]

I had written these few notes on her. A long time ago, not very long ago. I reproduce them in their severity, their clarity, their harshness.

1. Françoise Proust's essential 'classical' point of reference is probably Kant. There is, concerning Kant, a considerable body of work: introductions, editions and interpretations. Françoise Proust excels at bringing out what is really at stake in the most controversial texts (such as that on the question of

---

[*] Editorial note: Françoise Proust was a founding member of the Collège international de philosophie and author of numerous works, including *Kant, le ton de l'histoire* (1991), *L'histoire à contretemps: Le temps historique chez Walter Benjamin* (1994), *Point de passage* (1994) and *De la résistance* (1997).

[1] References in this chapter are to Proust's *Kant, le ton de l'histoire*, Paris: Payot-Rivages, 1991; and *De la résistance*, Paris: Le Cerf, 1997.

lying), and at displacing the emphasis in such a way that an essential but hitherto almost unnoticed motif justifies the reorganization of everything. As when she discerns in the *Critique of Pure Reason* the inaugural demand for a passive reception that is not just mere empiricity but which is itself *a priori* a sort of pathetic transcendental. That motif, as it happens, eventually becomes the main theme that runs through her entire undertaking. It is quite clear that her thought assumes the existence of a transcendental field. But what is constituted in that field belongs to neither the realm of knowledge nor that of the will. Her philosophical desire is basically attached to a transcendental theory of affect, or of the passions. One might almost say that the general title of what she was trying to establish is: Critique of Pure Passion.

2. As Heidegger has demonstrated, transcendental inspiration does not preclude, but calls for ontological theses. The same applies to Françoise Proust who, I maintain, outlines an ontology of the double, of the ambiguity of being, caught between the pure form of a 'state' and the activation – on, so to speak, the reverse side of that state – of a passivity that thwarts it, and which she calls counter-being. The way being is woven

together by that which maintains it and immanently thwarts it, is obviously especially difficult to decipher when it comes to the ontology of time. Within the framework of a ramified, fibred theory of time, which is articulated with a subtle reading of Walter Benjamin, she explains that time can be a name for both a continuity and a discontinuity, the name for the immanent deployment of that which *is* in terms of its conservative line, and the name of the evental strike that conjoins in time the precarious and the invisible.

3. When it comes to thinking the anti-dialectic of being and counter-being, the mediation is probably the activity/passivity doublet. All Françoise Proust's efforts go into establishing that positivity is on the side of the passive affect, on the side of that which receives the established order of being in the form of blows, and which by that very fact, deploys its own activity as a counter-blow, as a counter-attack, as resistance. Finding the rational *dispositif* in which affect is simultaneously the power of the 'counter', the invincibility of resistance, then leads her to Spinoza, whose whole investigation is, as we know, an attempt to think conjointly the active side of substance – *natura naturans* – and its passive side – *natura*

naturata – without having recourse to a theory of contradiction or negativity. Her reading of Spinoza is in fact filtered through Nietzsche, as reread by Deleuze and by Foucault. For once it is assumed that being is primarily power, the basic problem is to demonstrate that, far from being univocally on the side of the active force as such, creativity, inventiveness and the new are on the side of the activation of the reactive force. Detailed analyses of that activation give us both the starting point (indignation, anger, and a passive but also courageous reception of what is intolerable in the world), and the protocol. We then see the deployment of a dissymmetrical interplay of forces, as the cunning of resistance displaces the rules of the game, conjoining the most radical mobility and the most fixed immobility, and strives not so much to dominate the established power, as to disperse or disaggregate its component elements.

4. Having established her transcendental logic of power and affect, François Proust introduces convincing variations at three levels. At the historico-political level, she undertakes to demonstrate that it is resistance that explains active historicity, once we have understood that, whilst it is always localized and

punctual, that resistance is universal and ubiquitous because it is an immanent structure of being-power. But she also demonstrates that there are points inside 'great political events' where resistance crystallizes as such; they are recognizable because they are partisan dissidents operating within the general course of the sequence. For whenever the pre-established schemata of the active force try to stifle the resistance, there is resistance. There is resistance to the becoming of resistance. Hence the symptomatic significance of the crushing of the rebellion of the sailors in Kronstadt by the Bolsheviks, or the crushing of the Catalan anarchists by the orthodox Communists. Turning to war, she picks up Clausewitz's great analysis of the primacy of defence, sees it as the heritage of the theory of partisan warfare, and introducing into philosophy what is most contemporary, thinks the singularity of the Zapatista movement in Chiapas. Turning, finally, to life and death, and armed with experience and the profound knowledge it supports, Françoise Proust deploys a great philosophy of illness, demonstrating that illness can be thought only in terms of a truly strategic vision of life, which must not be approached as something that obviously exists, but as one of counter-being's precarious and subtle inventions.

5. What this work calls for is not of the order of academic judgements, but of that of evaluation and philosophical discussion. As I understand it, everything to do with the foundational level depends upon the ontological question of non-being.

The point of the recurrent image of the double is to guard against any lapse into the dialectic in the Hegelian sense. But there is no guarantee that one can easily avoid the dialectical nature of thought that is so firmly ensconced in the active/passive doublet. That doublet is itself problematic in so far as it obliges us to think being in the register of force or power, which is no doubt Françoise Proust's first option, or what we might call her ante-predicative option. If we wish to avoid a facile dualism, we then have to ascribe a force's active or passive nature directly to the relation of forces, as we see from the initial example of big fish chasing a little fish. It follows that, as Deleuze explicitly states, being is a relationship rather than a force. But it follows from that that resistance is not an intrinsic or immanent characteristic of force. It is a relative determination. But that relativity in its turn means that we cannot be sure that resistance as such deserves to be positivized. That much is obvious from the entire movement of Françoise

Proust's thought, and even more obvious from its tone. She is of course careful to say that resistance is of the order of being, and certainly not of the order of what-must-be. That she should choose this part of being as the only one that makes sense to her is no less striking. The question might also be introduced thus: how can we reconcile the assertion that resistance is rare, or precarious, with its truly logical basis in the immanent logic of counter-being? Basically, her whole project is to think being in such a way as to fuse in its constituent duplicity being in the true sense, or the being of being, and the event or the activation of counter-being, the passivity that is paralysed by the courage of the counter-attack. Personally, I do not think that such a fusion, which is supported by a logic of affect, can explain the sequential nature of truths, be they vital, artistic or political. I part company with Françoise Proust over the doctrine of being, which I believe to be undivided, and that of the event, which is not a counter-being or the structural double of being-as-state, but the hazardous suspension of one of the axioms of the multiple.

What does it matter, in the end? Resistant thought invents the law of its own movement.

We miss her now. I very often see, in this or that

situation, that we miss her. What we miss most is her excess. We really miss the very unpredictability of her fury. The strategic impatience that drove her to rush briskly towards a defeat that was of no importance, because the haste was all that mattered. We must read her, re-read her, in the hope that the enduring nature of these thoughts will be a sort of memorial to her absence. Like an everlasting flower on the blind stone of her absence.

A Note on the Texts

LACAN

This text appeared in the fortnightly *Le Perroquet*, which was founded by Natacha Michel and myself, and which was probably the most interesting paper published in the 1980s; the accuracy of that eulogy can be verified by reading the complete run (1981–87). Written just after the death of Lacan, the article appeared in the pilot issue of the fortnightly, dated November 1981.

I have written on, or about, Lacan very often. He is an essential point of reference for my first 'big' book on philosophy, *Théorie du sujet* (1982). In 1994–95, I devoted a whole year's seminar to him. In addition to the two sections of my systematic syntheses devoted to his thought in, respectively, the last and 38th mediation of *Being and Event* [*L'Etre et l'événement*, 1988] and *Logics of Worlds* [*Logiques du monde*, Book VII, section 2, 2006]. Long discussions, both admiring and critical, can be found in *Conditions* (1992), with particular reference to Lacan's relationship with the concept of the infinite, the notion of knowledge and the real experience of love. My most recent and complete text on the crucial question of Lacanian anti-philosophy appeared in English in the journal *Lacanian Ink* no. 27 under the title 'The Formulas of *L'étourdi*'.

CANGUILHEM AND CAVAILLÈS

This text appeared in no. 4 of the fortnightly *Le Perroquet*, dated February 1982. Canguilhem supervised my Master's thesis (known at the time as a *diplôme d'études supérieures*) on demonstrative structure in Spinoza's *Ethics*. My relationship with him then became more distant, especially after 1968. He did, however, speak highly of *Théorie du sujet* (1982). But he spoke ill of *L'Etre et l'événement*, writing to tell me that he 'had found no use for it'. When the Collège internationale de philosophie organized a colloquium in his honour in December 1990, I contributed a long paper, raising the question of whether his work delineated a particular concept of the Subject. He was kind enough to write to tell me that the text would be at the centre of his preoccupations. Those were his last words to me, and they were very kindly.

SARTRE

This is the text of a lecture given at the invitation of the UCFML (Union des communistes de France marxiste-léninistes), an organization in which I was active, at the University of Jussieu in Paris a few weeks after the death of Jean-Paul Sartre. The stated aim of the lecture was to swim against the tide of vague speeches and bids to grab all the credit, to outline a fairly rigorous evaluation of the philosophical debate between Sartre and Marxism and perhaps even between Sartre, History and Politics.

My starting point was the conviction that Sartre's master work on this subject (*Critique of Dialectical Reason*) was largely unknown to the people – mostly students – at the lecture. Hence the desire to be simple, to get to the point, whilst at the same time situating Sartre's intentions accurately. That was, in my view, an essential starting point if we wished to prevent Sartre, whose arguments dominated the progressive intelligentsia for a long period, from being remembered as nothing more than a vague institution.

Between 1981, the year in which this text was written, and now, I have regularly paid tribute to a man who was, when I was eighteen, my absolute master and the man who initiated me into the delights of philosophy. Much more recently an essential example of the abstract theory of 'points' (these are the moments when a subject formalizes a radical choice) in Book VI of *Logiques des mondes* is taken from Sartre's plays.

HYPPOLITE

This text is a transcription of my contribution to a day of commemorations (*Jean Hyppolite: entre structure et existence*) organized by the Centre internationale d'étude de la philosophie française contemporaine (CIEPFC) on 27 May 2006 at the Ecole normale supérieure, chaired by G. Bianco and F. Worms.

ALTHUSSER

This text was my contribution to the colloquium organized at the Université de Paris 8 by Sylvain Lazarus on 27 May 2002. The general title was 'Politique et philosophie dans l'oeuvre de Louis Althusser'. The proceedings were published by PUF in 1983. I subsequently spoke on Althusser on several occasions in France, but also in Brazil and Austria. A study that starts out from a different point of view can be found in my *Metapolitics* (Verso, 2005) [*Abrégé de métapolitique* (Seuil, 1998)] under the title 'Althusser: Subjectivity without a subject'.

Lyotard

This text was read at the collective tribute to Jean-François Lyotard organized by the Collège international de philosophie, and chaired by Dolorès Lyotard and Jean-Claude Milner, the Collège's director at that time. The proceedings were published by PUF in 2001 under the general title *Jean-François Lyotard, l'exercice du différend*.

Deleuze

This short text is taken from an issue of the *Magazine littéraire* devoted mainly to the tenth anniversary of the death of the philosopher.

Deleuze is probably the contemporary author on whom I have written most often, if somewhat late in the day: my *Deleuze: The Clamor of Being* [*Deleuze, la clamour de l'être*], which was commissioned by that magnificent editor Benoît Chantre, was published by Hachette in 1997. In *Logiques du monde*, a whole chapter (Book V, section 2) on the concept of the event is devoted to him. I regard him as the brilliant incarnation of a stance on all these questions that is the complete antithesis of my own. During the period of militant fury of the red years between 1966 and 1980, that took the form of violent opposition. Read my 'Le Flux et le parti', which I published in issue 6 of the journal *Théorie et politique* in March 1976: it transcribes a sort of fury. Much later, I learned to love Deleuze, but from within a controversy that would not die down. Platonism and anti-Platonism, basically.

Foucault
This text appeared in *Le Perroquet*, no. 42, July 1984, shortly after the death of Foucault.

Derrida
This text was read at the colloquium held to honour the memory of Jacques Derrida at the Ecole normale supérieure, 21–22 October 2005. A version had already been read at the University of California (Irvine). Another text for a friendship that took time to develop. The file on our serious disagreements has been made public, and can be found in an appendix to the proceedings of the *Lacan et les philosophes* colloquium published by Albin Michel in 1991. The